TRAVIS SENZAKI

How to Find your Best Degree Program and Advisor for the MEXT Scholarship

Mastering the MEXT Scholarship: The TranSenz Guide

First edition

ISBN: 978-4-909776-02-0

This book was professionally typeset on Reedsy.
Find out more at reedsy.com

For Sawa, Nina, Toma, and Emma

Contents

Preface

Hello and congratulations on your decision to apply for the Japanese Government Monbukagakusho (MEXT) Scholarship for research students!

I have been working with MEXT Scholarship applicants for a decade, first as the primary point of contact for all MEXT scholarship applicants at a large, private university in Japan, where I handled over 500 applications - only about 10% were successful - and since then, I have helped thousands of MEXT scholarship applicants through my blog, TranSenz. I based this book on my experience and research into the behavior of successful applicants to help give your application the best possible chance of success.

After all, as we covered in Book 1 of this series, *How to Apply for the MEXT Scholarship,* this scholarship is extremely competitive. There are only a few slots to go around, and you need to be better than the competition to secure the scholarship you deserve.

I hope that does not frighten you. Instead, I hope it motivates you. As I said: **You deserve this scholarship**. And you can earn it, if you are prepared to put in the work.

Finding the right advisor for your research in Japan is one of the most important parts of your scholarship application process. Not only is it an important part of getting accepted for the scholarship, but your relationship with your advisor over the course of your studies in Japan is one of the most important factors in your success and how much you enjoy your graduate school experience. It can have a lasting effect on your pursuit of your goals after graduation, too.

Of course, with all that to consider, and the challenges of finding information about programs and professors in Japan, this can be a rather stressful process for many applicants. My goal for this book is to take the stress out of the professor search by introducing a straightforward process for identifying and contacting potential advisors, to put the power in your hands.

I'm excited to be with you here on your journey. Now, let's get started.

Travis Senzaki
Akita, Japan
https://www.transenzjapan.com/blog/mext/

Getting Started

So, you want to apply for graduate school in Japan, and for the MEXT Scholarship to fund your studies? You're in the right place.

One of the most important steps in that process is choosing the university you want to apply to and the advisor that you want to study under. In some ways, this is like applying for graduate school in any other country, but there is one important difference that leaves hundreds, if not thousands, of MEXT Scholarship applicants feeling lost every year:

Lack of information.

Each year, hundreds of MEXT Scholarship applicants ask me some variation of the following questions:

- How do I find a university in Japan that teaches my field of study in English?
- Which university is best for my studies?
- How and when should I contact professors?

You may already know all of this for universities in your home country - or if not, you can find who does. But finding the same information about universities in Japan can seem like an impossible challenge. Well, not any more. Now you know someone. Now, you have all the information you need to find, reach out, and apply to universities in Japan in your hand.

It is still going to take some effort, but at you will be moving in the right direction.

How to Use This Book

This book is broken up into a preparation chapter and two halves. In the first half, I will introduce two methods for finding the best university-professor pair for your studies. In the second half, I introduce strategies for getting in touch with that professor and maintaining active communication to give you a better chance at getting accepted to the university.

How to Write a Scholarship-Winning Field of Study and Research Program Plan

This book is a companion to Book 2 of the Mastering the MEXT Scholarship Series: *How to Write a Scholarship-Winning Field of Study and Research Program Plan.*

To give yourself the best possible chance of winning the scholarship, researching universities and potential advisors should go hand-in-hand with developing your research plan. In *How to Write a Scholarship-Winning Field of Study and Research Program Plan,* I recommended your search for advisors should come after you complete your initial literature review and develop your research question.

I encourage you to get to that point before moving on to the chapters about identifying your potential universities and advisors in Japan. You will find it a lot easier to make the decisions in those chapters if you have a more specific idea of what you want to research. On the other hand, in order to avoid wasting effort, as soon as you have a research question, you'll want to make sure that you can indeed study that topic in Japan! You do not want to prepare a complete research plan only to find that there are no professors in

Japan working in the same field.

If you are using the two books together, then you'll want to go through the first half of this book - the parts about how to identify and evaluate universities and potential advisors - before going back to finish your Field of Study and Research Program Plan. Once you have finished that document, then you'll be ready to use the second half of this book to reach out to professors.

However, you do not need *How to Write a Scholarship-Winning Field of Study and Research Program Plan* to get value from this book. If you have already developed a research proposal or have your own method to do so, that will work just as well. Throughout this book, I will describe where you should be in your research process as you start each chapter, so that you can follow along.

Structure of the book

I encourage you to read each chapter, and complete the exercises as you go, in order to get the most out of this book. (The exception is Chapters 2 and 3, which describe two methods to reach the same goal.) But if you are up against a deadline and need to skip ahead, please use the descriptions below to guide you.

In the Preparation chapter, I will describe why this search is so important to your success as well as how to keep a clear focus on your goals throughout the search process. I will also cover the two key times for applicants to search for universities and advisors (spoiler: the two times are "in advance" and "at the last minute") and how your process should differ between the two.

Next, in the first half of the book, I will cover two methods to search for universities and advisors, as well as how to compare them to find the best choice for you. The goal of this section is to create a list of universities that you most want to study at, as well as your first-choice professor at each one.

For the Embassy-Recommended MEXT Scholarship, you will choose three universities and professors to write in the Placement Preference Form. For the University-Recommended MEXT Scholarship, you will apply to only one university and professor. However, in either case, you will want to have back-up options at this point in the application process.

There are two chapters in the first half, covering the two search methods, depending on whether you identify the university or the professor, first. In both chapters, as you compile your list of all the potential universities and professors, I will also introduce what factors you should look for in a professor that can be predictors of a successful advisor-advisee relationship.

After you compile that list, I recommend that you return to your Field of Study and Research Program Plan and write it targeting the first-choice professor from your list. Once you have done that, then return to this book to read the second half.

In the second half of the book, I will describe successful communication strategies to reach out to professors. We will start with the preparing for your initial outreach email. I will introduce strategies for planning your communication, cover expected email etiquette, describe specific tactics to find contact information, and explain how to write that initial email with sample templates. You will find strategies and specific email templates both for contacting professors in advance and at the last minute.

In the last chapter, I will also describe the different replies you might get and how to respond to them. By the time you get to that point of the book, you will be well on your way to establishing a long-term, successful relationship with your future advisor!

Of course, you may face some challenges along the way. You might struggle to find a professor that matches your research, or the communication process might not always go well. That's normal. Not everything will go according to plan. But if your research or communication reaches a dead end, return to the process and try again. The only way to fail is to give up, and I know you will not do that.

Downloadable Exercises

I have created a set of exercises and worksheets to accompany this book. The exercises help you put the lessons from each chapter into practice and will help you build up a list of the universities and professors that you want to apply to, narrow those down to your top choices, and prepare to write your initial contact emails. If you complete them as you read, then by the time you finish the book, you will already be in contact with your future advisor in Japan!

You can download the exercises from the link below. I will also include this link with each set of exercises, but I recommend you download them now. https://www.transenzjapan.com/mext/uniprofexercises

When you click that link, you will also sign up for a free companion email course that goes along with this book. Through that course, I will walk you through each of the chapters at a regular pace with additional encouragement for your application process.

(If you are reading the printed version of this book and cannot click the links included throughout the text, I have also included a list of links with those bonus documents!)

I will also email you if I have any updates to this book in the future or when I publish new articles or information about the MEXT Scholarship application process on my blog.

Definitions and Terminology

MEXT: The Japanese Ministry of Education, Culture, Sports, Science and Technology. If you put all of those letters together, you get MECSST, which is pronounced "MEXT".

You may also see the ministry called *Monbukagakusho* or *Monbusho*. The first is the official Japanese name and the second is the old Japanese name that still persists among former scholarship winners. All mean the same thing.

JASSO: The Japan Student Services Organization. JASSO is a quasi-governmental "Independent Administrative Institution" that supports MEXT's efforts. Their mission is to provide information about education in Japan in English and Japanese and also administer payment of government scholarships, including the MEXT Scholarship, on behalf of MEXT. JASSO also operates the "Study in Japan" website that we will use later in this book.

Research Student (*kenkyūsei*): When MEXT refers to the scholarship for "research students", they mean *kenkyūsei*. The better translation is "graduate students" and this term refers to all graduate-level students, whether enrolled in a degree-seeking program, or not.

In Japanese, each individual graduate school within a university is called a *kenkyūka,* or research division. *Kenkyū* means research, but this term translates as "graduate school" in almost all situations. For some reason *kenkyūsei,* which is derived from "student enrolled in a *kenkyūka*" translates as "research student".

Japanese translation inconsistency can be frustrating.

Research Student (*hiseikisei*): Universities use the term "research student" to refer to a student affiliated with a graduate school, but not enrolled in a degree program. As you can see, the word in Japanese is different, despite being translated into English with the same term as *kenkyūsei*. *Hiseikisei* means non-regular student and can refer to pre-graduate students who have not yet been admitted to the degree program or temporary students who have no intention of seeking a degree but just want to take courses and conduct research there.

Many MEXT scholarship winners, especially those who apply through the Embassy-Recommended MEXT Scholarship, start their studies in Japan as *hiseikisei* research students then matriculate to the degree program after arrival.

Degree-Seeking Student: A degree-seeking student is a student who has passed the entrance exam and matriculated into the degree program, as opposed to a *hiseikisei*. You can be a degree-seeking student at any level (undergraduate, masters, or doctoral). Once you are a degree-seeking student, you are "on the clock" to complete your degree within the designated standard number of years of enrollment: four for undergraduates, two for master's degrees, and three for doctoral degrees. (Exceptions exist for some degrees in medical fields that take longer.)

MEXT scholars who cannot complete their degrees within the designated standard years will lose the scholarship as soon as it becomes clear that they cannot complete on time.

Master's Degree: For this book, I will use the term Master's degree to encompass all master's level degrees, including academic and professional degrees. In Japan, academic degrees include Master of Arts or Master of Science degrees. There are also Master's-level professional degrees (see below) that fall under this category, such as MBAs and professional master's degrees in teaching.

Doctoral Degree: For this book, I will use the term Doctoral degree to encompass all doctorate level degrees, including academic and professional degrees.

5-year Doctoral Degree: Some programs in Japan offer a 5-year doctoral degree program with no Master's degree awarded in the interim. For the sake of the MEXT scholarship, you would still be a Master's level student for the first two years, even though you would not earn a degree after that point, and would have to apply for a scholarship extension to cover your participation in the final three years, which would be a doctoral degree, from MEXT's point of view.

If you have an appropriate Master's degree already, it may be possible to enter a 5-year Doctoral Degree from the third year of studies.

Professional Degree: Professional degrees are degrees that are required for a specific job qualification, rather than "pure" academic degrees. Examples include MBA, MD, MDDS, DVS, JD, DBA, etc. There is no prejudice against professional degrees within the evaluation system, but like anything else, you would have to justify why it is the most appropriate degree for your goal.

Embassy-Recommended MEXT Scholarship: Applying to the Japanese embassy or consulate in your home country for the MEXT scholarship. In this process, you will still need to contact universities later for Letters of Acceptance.

University-Recommended MEXT Scholarship: Applying to a university in Japan for the MEXT scholarship. In this process, you do not need to go through the Japanese embassy, except for your visa paperwork after selection.

Priority Graduate Program: This is a subset of the University-Recommended MEXT Scholarship. There are some university programs that are pre-approved by MEXT to nominate a specific number of students each year for the scholarship with the guarantee that all will receive it, if eligible. These programs often have very narrow eligibility requirements, for example, they may be limited to students with a particular nationality, in a specific degree program and level, and studying in a specific language. While the list of PGP programs is available, the eligibility criteria for each one are often not revealed, so it is hard to tell if you are eligible, even if the degree is in your field. If you meet the eligibility criteria for one of these programs, then your competition level is much lower and your chances of winning the scholarship skyrocket, but it is almost impossible to know in advance.

Primary Screening: The initial round of the application screening conducted at the embassy/consulate or university. This is the competitive round and determines who will earn recommendation to MEXT for the scholarship. Passing the primary screening almost guarantees that you will receive the scholarship.

Secondary Screening: MEXT's screening of recommended candidates. Although this screening takes longer than the Primary Screening, it is not competitive and it is rare for an applicant to lose the scholarship at this point. MEXT is just double-checking the embassy or university's work to make sure you are eligible. The application process is out of your hands at this point and there is nothing you can do but wait.

Placement Preference Form: One of the application documents that exists only in the Embassy-Recommended MEXT Scholarship application process. This is the form where you list the top three universities where you would like to enroll as well as your desired academic advisor at each one. The rest of this book focuses on identifying those universities and professors, then reaching out for initial contact.

Letter of Provisional Acceptance: A letter you have to obtain from universities in Japan after passing the Primary Screening for the Embassy-Recommended MEXT Scholarship. This letter states that the university will accept you if you are awarded the scholarship and also assigns an advisor. Each university will have it's own instructions for applying for this letter, which are separate from the general application process. Getting this letter is the point of this book, if you are applying from the Embassy-Recommended MEXT Scholarship!

Field of Study and Research Program Plan: The most important application document under your control. This is where you explain what you want to research in Japan and why. It is so important that I wrote Book 2 of this series, *How to Write a Scholarship-Winning Field of Study and Research Program Plan*, about that one form.

Graduation Thesis: This is the culminating paper or project for your degree. You will need to submit an abstract of your thesis for the screening process. At the undergraduate level, not all degree programs have a final thesis. That is fine. If you do not have a thesis or final project, check with the Embassy or University for guidance. They may ask you to submit an abstract of a term paper related to your research or tell that you do not need to submit anything.

Since the requirement is to submit an abstract, not the whole thesis, you can submit that even if you have not written the thesis yet.

When you contact universities and professors in Japan, your conversation will focus on your future research, but they may ask to see your current or past research, as well.

Visa: Japan uses the word "visa" in a different way from every other country

I am aware of. In Japan, a visa is only permission to enter the country. Once you arrive in Japan and pass through immigration, you have used up your visa and no longer have one (except with multiple-entry visas). Instead, you will have a Residence Status, which is your permission to stay in the country.

MEXT scholarship winners have a special student visa application process that bypasses the usual requirement to get a Certificate of Eligibility. You will receive more information about the process and specific instructions after selection, but you will only be able to get your student visa at the Japanese embassy or consulate in your home country that serves your place of residence.

Residence Status: Once you pass through immigration in Japan, your visa becomes invalid and you receive a residence status, instead. Your residence status is your legal permission to live in Japan to pursue the activities listed in that status. MEXT scholarship winners will have a Student Residence Status.

It is possible to change your residence status while living in Japan. For example, after graduating, you could apply to change your status to a working status. However, you cannot change your residence status *during* your MEXT scholarship award period or you will lose the scholarship.

CHAPTER ONE: PREPARATION

Before you search for universities and professors in Japan for your MEXT Scholarship, you need to understand why this process matters - and why it matters to you. In this preparation chapter, I will describe the first part and walk you through the second.

Where You Should Be

You can read this chapter any time, but you will get the most benefit out of it if you have already prepared yourself to start your search for universities and professors in Japan.

Before starting this chapter, you should have a clear goal for how you want to contribute to society after completing your MEXT scholarship and understand how your research in Japan is essential to that goal. (Establishing these goals was the subject of Book 1 in this series, *How to Apply for the MEXT Scholarship.*) It would be better if you have also developed your (draft) specific research question before reading onward, as I described in the first half of Book 2, *How to Write a Scholarship-Winning Field of Study and Research Program Plan.* You do not need your research question for this chapter, but you will need it before starting your search for universities and professors in Chapter 2 or 3.

If you're ready, read on!

WHY YOUR SEARCH MATTERS

Your relationship with your academic advisor in Japan is the most important factor in the success or failure of your studies. It is not something that you can afford to leave to chance. I know this from my experience and past MEXT scholars agree.

When I applied for graduate school, one of my mistakes was picking a program because of its course selection and scholarship availability, without giving serious thought to my advisor or research. I was pursuing a master's degree in Japanese studies, and I figured that as long as the university had the courses I wanted, I could figure the rest out later.

It didn't go well.

My program assigned an advisor during my first year, and I think I saw him twice outside of his mandatory class. When I chose a thesis advisor in the second year, I only ended up seeing him when I submitted my thesis for his review prior to my defense. Neither of them offered any help, and I didn't feel like I could ask them. So, when I got discouraged or confused in my research, I had nowhere at that university to turn for help. I finished my degree frustrated and wanting nothing more than to get away from academia.

And that is just an example of a non-existent advisor relationship. Imagine what would have happened if we'd had a negative relationship!

Finding an advisor whose research relates to your interest and who can provide advice and encouragement along the way is essential. You want someone that you will be comfortable working with or talking to, both when you are excited about your research and when you are struggling. Your search for a university and professor in advance, plus reaching out to build a relationship before you apply, can go a long way to ensuring that successful and supportive environment.

Past MEXT scholars that I have talked to are almost unanimous in recommending that you contact potential advisors in advance to see if you can establish rapport and a supportive relationship. The only way to know if you will be able to work with this advisor long term is to interact directly to find out if your advisor is passionate about their research and supportive of yours, as well as whether they are internationally minded. If not, then you want to find out while you still have time to consider an alternative university and advisor.

Some of the work we will go through in the rest of this book may seem tedious. I will recommend that you create a long list of universities and professors and research each one to determine who you want to approach. But I hope you understand how important this process is to ensuring your success with the academic research you want to complete in Japan in the first place!

PRACTICAL CONSIDERATIONS

Beyond the quality of your relationship, contacting a professor in advance is important to ensure that they can supervise you. You do not want to put all of your effort into applying for a university just to learn that the only professor in your field cannot supervise you because they are retiring, or they cannot take on additional advisees, etc. Contacting professors in advance can ensure you do not experience an unpleasant surprise when you go to submit your formal application.

Of course, saying all of this, I know that some of you reading this book are up against a deadline. In that case, you won't have the time to reach out and evaluate professors through personal contact. But the research steps I describe over the next few chapters are still going to help you narrow down your advisor search to have the best possibility of success, so I encourage you to follow as many of these steps as you have time to do.

KNOW YOUR GOALS

Your relationship with your advisor matters because it will be one of the most important factors in determining whether you achieve your research goals in Japan. But what are your goals?

If you have read my previous book, *How to Apply for the MEXT Scholarship,* you'll remember my recommendation that you build your entire application around specific practical and academic goals. You need to know what you are aiming to do in your first five years after graduation and how your studies in Japan will contribute to your goal before you consider universities. Different universities and different professors may be in a better position to help you toward different goals, even within the same research field.

Your goals can also help you narrow down your target universities before you even begin researching potential advisors. Based on your goals, you can decide what university characteristics are important to you. For example, does the university's location matter? Its size? If you are going to consider any of those factors, make sure you understand how they relate to your goals.

Here are a few examples of university characteristics and how they might affect your goals:

1. Size:
   A larger university will typically have more resources for research facilities and be able to support your research with conference funding, etc., but you may feel overwhelmed and alone as one of many students. At a smaller university, it is often easier to establish relationships and

get more personal support. Also consider that at universities with fewer graduate schools each school will get a larger proportion of the funding, so even if there are fewer resources, it may be easier to obtain them.

2. Location:

The most important reason location would be a factor would be if it relates to your research. But there are other considerations, such as the living environment, too. If you are conducting research on a specific site, group of people, company, or environment, then it makes sense to be located close to that research subject. For example, if your research involves corporate management strategies at Japan's top brands, you'll want to be close to those companies' headquarters. However, if you are researching their technological innovations, it would make more sense to be closer to their factories or R&D facilities. Of course, you can travel for your research if you have to, but you are also more likely to find professors who have similar research to yours at universities that are close to your research subject.Living environment and cost of living could also be factors. It is possible to live on a MEXT Scholarship stipend alone, even in Tokyo, if you are frugal. But for MEXT scholars who want to bring their spouses and children to Japan and do not have other sources of income, that stipend will go a lot further in a rural area. Living environments can also vary between different cities and between urban and rural areas. I have found without fail that rural communities in Japan are much more warm and welcoming, so if getting involved in the community is important to you, then consider getting out of the city. On the other hand, there are more English-speakers in cities, which could make life easier for you. Consider what factors are most important to you.

3. University Ranking:

I think university ranking is almost worthless, but that is just my opinion. Most of the factors that go into university ranking have little to do with what your experience at that university will be like as a scholar. However, top-ranked universities attract top-level students, so at a ranked university, your fellow scholars would be more likely to be driven and at the top of their field. That could offer better networking opportunities, as well as a university community that will push you toward excellence. Top-ranked/well-known universities can also provide an advantage if you are planning to look for work in Japan after graduation or if you are planning to go into a career in academia, since the rank of your university could be a factor in the hiring process. However, top-ranked universities can sometimes be cold and arrogant toward students during the application process.If you are going to look at ranking, I would recommend that you look at the ranking for your specific research field. If a university has a high rank, but it is because of a different field of study, then expect that the university will focus its resources (money and personnel) on that field, and your research might be at a lower overall priority.

My point in explaining these factors is not to persuade you to choose one type of university over another. It is to make sure that, if you look at these factors, you understand what they mean to you and to your goals. That is why it is important to know your goals before you go any further with this search. In later chapters, I will talk about when and how to apply these factors, but I encourage you to consider what is important to you now, before we move forward.

If you have already read *How to Apply for the MEXT Scholarship,* take some time to go back now and look at what you wrote in your exercises for chapter 4, where we developed your goals. If you haven't read that book, or didn't complete the exercises, I have included a shortened version of the goal development questions in the exercise for this chapter.

WHEN TO SEARCH AND CONTACT

There are two primary times when MEXT Scholarship applicants search for potential universities and advisors in Japan:

1. Before starting their application or research proposal, or
2. While filling in the application documents and up against a deadline.

I assume you know I recommend the first one, if you have time. But you cannot go back in time if you are in the second situation while reading this. Throughout the rest of this book, I will provide advice for each timeline where they differ.

If You are Preparing in Advance

Researching and getting in contact with universities and professors in advance is ideal, if possible. But when should you do it?

I'll offer my idea of the contact "sweet spot", but there are going to be individual factors that go into your decision. So, please do not treat the suggestions below as rigid guidelines. For example, if you get introduced to a particular professor, through a mutual connection or during a study abroad experience in Japan, and that is a professor that you are interested in working with, start communicating with them right away to maintain that relationship. (Of course, in that case, you don't need this book!)

But let's assume for now that you do not have a direct connection with a professor in Japan and are starting this search from scratch. When is the best time to reach out? There are a few factors to consider, including your preparedness, how long you have to the application period, and how comfortable you are maintaining communication.

Preparedness

If we only consider preparedness, then you should search for and contact professors as soon as you are ready. But what does that mean?

If you read book 2 in this series, *How to Write a Scholarship-Winning Field of Study and Research Program Plan,* you'll remember that I suggested you research universities and professors in Japan as soon as you have completed your initial literature review and have a draft research question that you will pursue in Japan. At that point in the research process, you want to stop and make sure that there are professors in Japan who can supervise your research. If not, it would be time to change your research question to one that you can pursue in Japan.

So, you are "ready" to *research* universities and professors in Japan as soon as you have that draft research question. But that is not time to *contact* them. I recommend you finish writing your Field of Study and Research Program Plan, based on your research of professors in Japan, and only contact them once you have a completed plan you could submit.

When that happens is up to you and when you prepare for the application.

Time until the application period

I suggest that you be in contact with professors before the application period opens. If you contact them for the first time during the application period, then understand that they may receive many requests from other MEXT scholarship applicants at the same time. Because you are reading this book, you are going to be more prepared for the application than most others out there, but if you contact professors during a busy time, there is a higher chance they will consider you with everyone else, so you may not get as much of their time and attention.

In a typical year, MEXT posts the Embassy-Recommended MEXT Scholarship Application Guidelines around mid-April. The Primary Screening and the time for requesting letters of acceptance from universities goes until August. For the University-Recommended MEXT Scholarship, the application period varies by university, but October through December is a common time.

So, if we consider those schedules, then you would want to get in contact with professors by January to February of the year that you plan to submit your application. (Avoid March if you can. Most universities are out of session then between academic years, so your chances of getting replies from professors will be lower).

That's when you want to get in *contact*. Since you want to give yourself plenty of time to write your Field of Study and Research Program plan, you'll want at least one month and preferably two to three between when you do your initial research of professors and when you contact them.

That moves your research back to around November of the year before you plan to apply.

Of course, if you are already past that time, do not despair. This is just an ideal schedule and you can make this work within a shorter timeline. As long as you prepare now and do your research and contact as soon as possible, you will still give yourself a better chance to get in contact with professors, build a relationship, and ensure that you can secure acceptance to the university when the time comes.

Comfort with long-term communication

This one is going to be based on your personality. Every year, applicants ask me, "Once I've gotten in touch with my potential supervisor in advance, what do I do to maintain that relationship?" That is an excellent question, and I will cover it later in the communication strategy section toward the end of the book. But for now, understand that once you get in touch with the professor, it is going to be necessary to nurture that relationship through continued communication.

Are you prepared to maintain a relationship via regular emails with your potential advisor in Japan over a period of several months or a year? If not, then consider contacting the professor closer to the application period, rather than farther in advance.

Do not worry that you are going to have to be in contact daily or anything like that, but consider that once you have established a relationship, you should keep in touch at least monthly, with a focus on your research.

So, what's your sweet spot?

The ideal time for you to contact professors (and, by extension, to research them) is going to change based on your individual circumstances and possibilities. For now, you need to understand your ideal timing and start planning accordingly. There are a few questions in the exercises at the end of this chapter that will help with that process.

After the Application Process Begins

If you are reading this after the application process has started, or perhaps after the Primary Screening, do not let that last section bother you. Yes, it is ideal to contact professors well in advance, but that does not mean that your application will fail if you do not. It just means that you have to work harder now to compress all the research, vetting, and communication into a shorter span.

After the application process starts, there are two key times to consider contacting potential advisors.

Before submitting your application

Even if the application process has started, it would be ideal to get in touch with potential advisors in Japan before applying to the embassy or university, if you can.

Just like I described in the section about preparing in advance, I recommend you research your potential advisors after you have developed your initial research question and start contacting them after you have a Field of Study and Research Program Plan you are ready to submit to the embassy or university for the application. Those are your two key steps and the timing.

Please remember, though, that just because you might be in a rush at this point since you have a deadline looming, you cannot rush the professors. It is not necessary to contact professors before passing the Primary Screening for the Embassy-Recommended MEXT Scholarship, and they are under no obligation to reply to you. Some universities even have a policy to not reply to applicants who have not yet passed the Primary Screening! So, you'll need to be prepared for silence on their part. In that case, you'll need to decide whether to try another professor or wait and contact them again after passing the Primary Screening.

Of course, if you are applying for the University-Recommended MEXT Scholarship, there may be a requirement by the university to contact professors in advance. In that case, make sure you are following their instructions to the letter!

I will cover how you want to contact professors at this point in the application timeline later, in the chapter on making initial contact.

After passing the embassy Primary Screening

Start contacting universities and professors as soon as you receive your Passing Certificate of the Primary Screening.

Why not reach out earlier?

I do not recommend contacting universities or professors for the first time between when you have submitted your application and the end of the Primary Screening. The Primary Screening is the most competitive part of the application process, when the vast majority of applicants are eliminated. Universities and professors know this, and they know that while a post-Primary Screening applicant has a near certain chance of earning the scholarship, anyone who has not passed that screening yet is a wild card. You may even find some universities have a no-contact policy during this time. I'm not saying it's forbidden or that you can't try it, but you are more likely to meet with frustration if attempting first contact before passing the Primary Screening.

Of course, continue your research on potential universities and professors during this time. Since you have not contacted professors yet, you are going to need more back-up options when it comes time to reach out. Do not worry about what you wrote in your Placement Preference Form, even if you have already submitted it. You should be able to change it later.

If you are applying for the Embassy-Recommended MEXT Scholarship, then after the Primary Screening is the first time you must contact universities and/or professors. Since this is part of the required process, you will need to make sure you know how each university wants you to apply for the Letter of Acceptance and follow those directions.

Again, I will cover your approach to contacting universities and professors in the chapter about making initial contact.

HOW TO SEARCH FOR UNIVERSITIES AND PROFESSORS

We've discussed "why" and "when" to search, but I assume that the most important question on your mind is "how". I will cover that in the next two chapters, but for now, here is a summary to help you prepare to make the most of the next sections.

In this search process, your goal will be to create a list of university-professor pairs. A university-professor pair is the name of a university where you could consider applying and *one* professor there that you would want to supervise you. At first, you should create as long and extensive a list as possible, since that will give you a better chance of finding an ideal situation and will also offer back-up plans in case your top choices do not work out.

You can create this list starting with the university first and professor second, or the other way around. In the next two chapters, I will introduce both methods. You do not need to follow both, but choose the method that makes the most sense to you and create your list that way.

Searching for universities first means that you'll be sure that you are only considering programs taught in English, which narrows your search. You might have to think broadly about your research field, since the terminology in Japan could differ from what you're used to. Every year, I have a few applicants contact me in a panic because they cannot find any universities in Japan that offer programs in their field. However, it is almost always a case of using different names for the same field or searching for too narrow of a sub-field at first.

I recommend this search method for applicants whose fields are not widely available in English in Japan or for applicants who do not need as close a relationship between their research and their advisor's. For example, applicants in social sciences and humanities can find benefit in this approach. Those fields offer a little more flexibility in the relationship between scholars' and advisors' fields of study, and there are fewer universities that offer them in English in Japan.

Applicants whose last university has many partners in Japan and who want to start by approaching these partner universities can also benefit from a university-first search!

The second method involves searching for professors first. In this approach, you'll have an easier time finding professors whose research interest is closer to your own, since there are better keyword research tools available and you won't have to guess as much about program names. The disadvantage is that you may find that the professor you want to work with teaches at a university that does not offer programs taught in English.

I recommend the professor-first search for applicants in STEM fields. In those fields, you will often be part of a professor's laboratory and working on a subset of the professor's research. So, it is more important that both your research subject and methods match with your professor. STEM fields are also more commonly offered in English in Japan than humanities and social sciences, so you are less likely to find a "perfect" professor, only to find that they are in a Japanese-only program.

Of course, you can choose either method - or both - regardless of your field! The recommendations above are only guidelines. I will describe the pros and cons of each method in more detail in the following chapters.

Once you have completed your university-professor list, regardless of the method, our next step will be a comparative analysis of each of the pairs to determine which is best for you. This is also when you will consider factors related to your goals as discussed earlier. So, do not eliminate any options until you get to that point.

PROGRESS CHECK

In this chapter, we have gone through the why and when of your search, as well as the beginnings of how.

You should understand now just how important it is to find the best possible university and professor in Japan to meet your research goals. You should have also gone through and listed those goals (if you haven't, please complete the exercises before moving on. I cannot overstate how important it is to make sure your actions align with your goals!)

We also reviewed the two different times for researching and contacting professors, so you know what group you fall into. That will affect how you approach your research and contact later.

Finally, I described the process of creating and evaluating a university-profe ssor pair list, including the two methods for compiling that list.

With all that talk about what's coming next, I am sure that you are eager to get started with the actual process of researching universities and professors! Or, perhaps, you're feeling intimidated by the task ahead of you? In either case, whether you are excited or nervous, the best thing you can do is to take the first small, practical steps.

In the next two chapters, I will discuss the two methods for compiling the university-professor list, including the search resources and what to look for. Start with whichever method appeals most to you, but feel free to try both as well.

EXERCISES

I highly recommend that you download the free exercise worksheets I have created, print them, and fill in the questions there as you read through the book. While some exercises might work best as a spreadsheet (I will mention that where relevant), there is something powerful about writing out your goals by hand that makes you more likely to achieve them.

https://www.transenzjapan.com/mext/uniprofexercises

Whether you handwrite or type, do not simply keep your answers to these questions in your head. Write them down. Writing your thoughts gives them power. It will help you move forward, commit to a course of action, and make progress toward your goals.

Your goals

This is a condensed version of the exercises that appear in chapter four of *How to Apply for the MEXT Scholarship*. If you completed the exercises there, you can refer to those, instead.

1. Goals: How do you want to serve the world and society after graduation

(what field of endeavor will you contribute to)?

2. Goals: What is one practical contribution to that field that you can realistically make within the first five years after graduation?

3. Goals: Visualize yourself at the point of graduation. What are you going to do next? Where will you work (or study)? What kind of work do you aim to do there?

4. Goals: What do you need to get out of your MEXT scholarship degree in order to prepare to be the version of yourself that you visualized? Make a list of the most important results to you.

5. Goals: Does your research in Japan require you to be in, or close to, a specific location in Japan?

6. Goals: Does your life situation make a particular location better for you than others? (e.g. family and cost of living, proximity to major airport, healthcare needs, living environment).

7. Goals: Start with university size, location, and ranking, and think about how each could affect your specific goals and personal situation. List the results below, then decide what factors are important to you, and how important they are. Is there anything on your list that is potentially more important to you than your relationship with your future advisor?
   Size:
   Location:
   Ranking:

Contact timing

8. When will your application period start? (Typically April of the year before you want to start your studies for the Embassy Application or October of the year before you want to start your studies for the University Application).

9. How much time do you have before that start date, in months?

10. Have you developed your research question? If not, when can you have that research question developed?

11. Have you finished your Field of Study and Research Program Plan? If not, when will you have that done?

12. Are you comfortable maintaining a long-distance professional relationship by email?

13. Based on all the factors above, when do you plan to contact professors?

14. Giving yourself one to three months before the contact date above, when will you research universities?

CHAPTER TWO: HOW TO SEARCH BY UNIVERSITY

Are you ready to get to work?

In this chapter, I will cover the first of the two methods I recommend to create a list of university-professor pairs. You only need to use one of the two methods, so before we get started, I want to summarize how this method works and who it works best for, so you can choose whether to try this approach or starting with professors, as described in the next chapter.

But first. . .

Where you should be

You should already know what you want to research in Japan, and why, before you create your list of university-professor pairs.

In the last chapter, I discussed the importance of knowing your goals. Make sure you understand what you want out of the MEXT Scholarship before starting your search. During this search process, you are going to be looking at the possibilities available in Japan. If you are anything like me, some of the research and fields of study you come across will seem exciting and you may be tempted to change your research area or broaden your focus.

Don't do that.

I get it, a new idea can seem shiny and exciting compared to something you have been working on for a while. New ideas can be tempting as you go through the laborious process of working out your research question and creating your research plan. The initial stage of exploration can be a lot more fun. But do not lose sight of your original goal and the work you have put in so far.

Speaking of the work that you have put in so far, you should also have a research question written out before starting your search for universities and professors. At the very least, you should have a research problem you want to explore.

OVERVIEW OF SEARCHING BY UNIVERSITY

Before you make your list, I want to describe the process and who it might work best for, so that you can decide if you want to use this approach or search by professor, as we'll cover in the next chapter. I touched on this in the Preparation chapter, but here it is in more detail.

Your first step will be to create a list of all the universities in Japan that offer graduate programs where you could complete your research. At this point, all you have to go on is the general field of the graduate program, like "history" or "life sciences". (I also have some suggestions about how to think about these program names.) This is like a brainstorming phase where you will list all the possibilities and not eliminate anything.

Next, you will visit each university's home page to look at the program and see if they have a department or major that covers your specific interest. For example, if your research question had to do with the Meiji Restoration period in Japan, you'd want to make sure that the history programs you found have a focus in 19th century Japanese history and eliminate those that don't meet your needs.

Finally, in the third phase, you'll be looking at specific professors in each program to identify the one who is best able to supervise your research. Again, you'll be adding data to your list. This time, the focus will be on prioritization rather than elimination, but there could be some of the latter, as well.

By the end of this process, you will have a list of universities with programs taught in English in your field and the name of the professor there who is best able to supervise your research.

Benefits of this approach

Overall, this is the most straightforward search method, which is why I list it first. You start with the broad field and work your way down to the narrow. If you like a reliable, methodical approach, this will work well for you.

This method is also comprehensive. Since we start with a list of all the possibilities and then eliminate them, there is very little chance that you'll be missing any opportunities.

It can help you clarify a vague research problem. I recommended having your research question or problem on paper before you start your search, but I recognize that is not always the case for all applicants. If you do not have a research problem yet, just a goal to earn a degree in a particular field, then this approach will help you find the possibilities in your field, as well as information about research going on in Japan, so that you can decide on your research problem and question before you move on.

Searching by university can be the better approach when your research in Japan does not have to relate precisely to your academic advisor's. This is often the case in humanities and social sciences fields, at least at the master's level. It is still helpful to find an advisor whose research specialty is similar enough to your own that they can offer advice about resources, but you have more flexibility with related fields or similar methodologies.

Searching by university can minimize the possibility of disappointment. When you search by professor, you may find a professor who is ideal to be your advisor, only to learn that they are not affiliated with a program taught in English. If you start with programs taught in English, you can avoid getting emotionally invested in a match that might be impossible.

Finally, searching by university allows you to start with partner universities, where your application can have a greater chance of success. One approach I will introduce later in this chapter is to start your search with universities in Japan that have a partnership with your current university. A partnership can mean that there is a personal connection you can leverage with that university and, in the case of the University-Recommended MEXT Scholarship, it can be critical to your application - indeed, some Japanese universities only accept applications from partner university students!

These are the chief advantages to starting your search for university-profess or pairs with the university, but there are also some comparative drawbacks and limitations that might make you want to choose a professor-first search. I will explain those below.

Limitations of this approach

Being methodical and comprehensive means that this approach can also be time-consuming. You will end up spending a lot of time researching programs that do not end up on your list. This can still be beneficial, since you will be more knowledgeable on the state of your field in Japan, but if you are under time pressure as you read this, that could be a challenge.

You might miss some peripheral opportunities for cross-field research with a program taught in Japanese. This is a rare situation, but I have worked with applicants in the past who wanted to work with a professor that was in a Japanese-only program (e.g. pharmaceutical science), so they enrolled in a related English-taught program (e.g. life sciences) at the same university and consulted with that professor throughout their research.

Searching by university can lead to dead ends if you have a specific research question in mind already, especially if your field requires a close match with your professor. Since you are starting broad and working your way to narrow, the time you have to put into researching each program can be significant before you learn if it matches your needs or not.

Which method will you choose?

If you have reviewed the pros and cons above and want to continue with searching by university, read on! Over the rest of this chapter, I will walk you through that process.

If you decide you want to search by professor first, instead, skip to the next chapter. You can always come back as necessary, or even use both methods!

In either case, your goal for now will be to create a list of all university-p rofessor pairs for your studies in Japan, then prioritize it. So, for now, I encourage you to treat this step like a brainstorm and come up with as many options as possible. Once you contact potential supervisors, later in this book, you might find that you need to change your priorities or switch to a new target, so try to have more options on your list than you need. Do not start eliminating yet!

In the bonus documents, I have included a template spreadsheet that you can use to track all the university data that you research, so I recommend you download it, if you have not yet done so.

STEP 1: CREATING A LIST OF PROGRAMS

Your goal in this process is to create a list of university-professor pairs, but in this method, we are starting with the university. So the first step is to create a list of all the English-taught programs in your general field.

During this part of the process, you are going to be using external resources, rather than information from the universities themselves, so you cannot get specific information about the programs, yet. That's fine for now.

There are four resources I recommend for searching for programs taught in English in Japan. Three are websites, but the fourth is your own current university. I will explain each of them below.

Japan Student Services Organization (JASSO)

https://www.studyinjapan.go.jp/en/planning/search-school/

This is the most comprehensive list, though it is not the most detailed or visually pleasing.

JASSO is a quasi-governmental organization and is best known amongst international students for administering scholarships, including payments for the MEXT Scholarship.

Each year, JASSO contacts universities to request that they update their lists of programs taught in English. Universities do not need to reply, but most universities who want to attract international students will, so this is the most complete and up-to-date list.

To use this resource, access the link above, then click the link on the site for "Degree Courses Taught in English". That will take you to a pdf file showing all the degree courses that you can complete entirely in English. The PDF is broken down by field of study, then sub-field. For example, as of early 2021, the first field is "Humanities", which is broken into several subcategories, starting with "Literature".

This list also shows whether the university is national, local public, or private, the name of the specific program or course as well as the school or graduate school, and the degree levels available in English. Some courses also show that they are not entirely available in English, but if they are on this list, then you should be able to complete the degree program without having to take courses in Japanese (I'll explain how to check that later). Even if a course shows that the language is "E>J", meaning that some courses are in Japanese, that should still mean you can complete the degree in English, but there might be some courses taught in Japanese that you cannot enroll in.

This site is only going to give you the name of the university and course (i.e. program/department). Sometimes, that program name will not be precise about what it includes (for example, at the time of writing, Waseda University only lists the name of the graduate school and "English based degree program" for each program in the list.) That's fine for this first step. Add it to the list. We will check the university's website for more details in the next step of the search.

Since there are no details here, my advice is to start with a broad search - look for as many programs as possible that *might* cover your field of interest. Your particular field might be too narrow to be listed here by itself, but in that case, do not give up! Think about what a broader field could be. For example, if you cannot find "petroleum engineering", look for "engineering" programs, instead. Later, you can check the website for the individual programs to see if they offer a major or subfield in petroleum engineering.

Also, do not stop when you think you have found your field. You may find other related fields if you continue to scroll down. For example, there is a section for "Biology", then another one later for "Applied Biology", then "Biotechnology", "Bioproduction and Bioresources", "Comprehensive Sciences", etc. There is no particular order to this document, so be sure to read to the end.

List every program that you think might be relevant. You can use the downloadable spreadsheet to help you.

Japan Study Support (JPSS)

http://www.jpss.jp/en/univ/english/

JPSS is a site run by a private corporation, Benesse, in cooperation with the Asian Students Cultural Association. Benesse is involved in higher education in Japan, including annual surveys and being the local partner for the Times Higher Education ranking of Japanese universities. JPSS also provides some scholarships.

The JPSS website has a partial list of programs taught in English in Japan, but they are not as proactive as JASSO in reaching out to universities or updating their information. They offer a platform that universities can use, if they wish, to provide information about their programs.

While this site is not as complete, it offers more information on each of the universities listed, so you can get an overview of the university before deciding on whether to add it to your list. Keep in mind, however, that this website is for applicants to fee-paying programs, so not all the information you find on admissions information, etc., will apply to you as a MEXT scholar.

This site is best used for browsing, rather than for a particular search. I recommend scrolling down the list. Each entry will describe the university, which is not useful or relevant, and include a list of programs taught in English that they want to advertise. That list should be your focus.

Just like we did for the JASSO list above, look for any programs here that might cover your field and add them to your list. You can also click the "More Information" link for further program details to help you decide whether it is a good fit, and there are links to the university websites, as well. I recommend bookmarking those links if you don't read them right away, since the next step after making this list will be to review the program details on the university websites.

Univ In Japan

https://univinjapan.com/

Like JPSS, above, this site is run by a private corporation and universities choose whether to keep their information posted and up-to-date here. It is going to be a more limited list than JASSO, but it also means that the universities listed here have taken that extra step to reach out to international students!

This site also has a list feature, which you can find by clicking "List of Universities", then "Postgraduate Programs", but the search function on the home page, or accessible through the "Postgraduate Program Search" tab in the menu, is what makes UNIV in Japan easiest to use. You can narrow down the list of potential options here for further exploration!

There are also features to narrow your search by region of Japan and type of institution, but I do not recommend using those at the beginning. Your goal should be to find the best possible university and research situation for yourself, and you do not want to limit your search by using criteria that do not serve that goal.

Additional Websites

I should also mention that I have an article on my blog about searching for universities and professors. Of course, it does not go into as much detail, but if I discover additional resources for this search process later, I will add them to that article. So, if you are reading this book well after the original publication, it would be worth checking that out to see if there are any new resources there:

"How to Find Universities and Professors in Japan"
https://www.transenzjapan.com/blog/how-to-find-universities-and-professors-in-japan-mext-scholarship/

University Partnerships

As promised, the fourth resource here is not a website, but your own university's international partnership office.

By your own university, I mean the university where you are enrolled as a degree-seeking student, or the university that you graduated from most recently. If that university has any partners in Japan, it is worth your time to check if those Japanese universities have programs taught in English in your field.

Why a partnership matters

A formal partnership relationship between your university and the university in Japan can improve your application chances in several ways.

The first way is name recognition. When Japanese universities are receiving a deluge of applications, either for Letters of Acceptance from Embassy-Recommended MEXT Scholarship applicants or for the University-Recommended MEXT Scholarship, it helps to be from a university that will stand out in the reviewers' minds. If there is a formal partnership between your universities, they will be more familiar with the quality of your university and may even feel a sense of obligation to give your application a more thorough consideration.

The second way a partnership can help you is, if there is actual interaction between the universities, you may leverage that connection to reach out to your target professor, when we get to that part of the book.

The third benefit is that for the University-Recommended MEXT Scholarship, some Japanese universities will only accept applications from students from their partner universities abroad. They may even recruit through those universities and not publish a public call for applications on their own websites at all.

This is not an exhaustive list of benefits of a relationship, but I hope it is enough for you to understand why it would be valuable to give extra consideration to partner universities in Japan.

I would even say that if you are starting your MEXT application preparation early enough - such as a year before you apply - you might even want to encourage your university to establish a partnership with Japanese universities and try to help in that process!

How to find partnerships

Partnerships between universities can exist at different levels, but partnerships at the university-wide level or at the faculty level are the most common. If your university has a central international office or division, or a Vice-Provost of Internationalization or similar role, I would recommend checking there, first. They can tell you about any university-wide partnerships and should also know what other offices at the university manage their own partnerships, if any.

I mentioned one level of partnerships is a faculty-level, but that doesn't have to be your faculty! For example, if your university's faculty of science and engineering has a partnership with a Japanese university, but you are majoring in history, that's fine. It's still a partnership between universities and counts for our purposes. Of course, if the partnership is in a different field, that means that there is less chance that the Japanese university has a program taught in English in your field or that there will be a direct relationship you can leverage. But you would still have the benefit of name recognition at the Japanese university!

How to list partner universities

In every other step in this section so far, we have looked at lists of programs that were taught in English. For the partnership-centered search, though, there is no guarantee that the Japanese university will have a program taught in English in your field, so I would recommend making a separate list of these programs, or leaving a space in your list to separate them from the programs you have already listed that you know to be in English.

If you find a partnership with a university that was already on your list of English programs, that's great! Mark that university with a star and consider prioritizing it in your search, at least until you see how related the program and its professors are to your research interest.

Our next step for all universities that you have listed so far will be to review the university and program's websites, so at that point we'll also check if your partner universities have programs taught in English.

STEP 2: RESEARCH THE PROGRAMS

In Step 1, we created a long list of all the possible programs taught in English in Japan that might meet your research goals. At that point, I advised you to keep everything on your list and to not eliminate any potential options.

Now it is time to change gears. In Step 2, we will be prioritizing and eliminating programs to create a short list to carry into the final step of your search.

During this step, your primary resource is going to be the websites of the university programs that you have listed so far. If you already have the website links from the last step, that will make your search faster, but if not, you should be able to find the sites easily enough with a quick Google search.

As you review each site, here's what I suggest you look for:

- Relevance of the program to your research interest
- Quality of information available in English
- Factors related to your goals and constraints

I will explain each of these search criteria in more detail below.

I recommend using a three-tiered scoring system and giving each university a score for each criterion. In Japan, a common system is a circle for "yes", a triangle for "maybe" and an X for "no", but you can use whatever makes most sense to you. In any case, by the time you finish this process, you should have a clear picture of how to prioritize your university list.

You can continue to use the spreadsheet from the bonus documents for this process and add additional columns to it if necessary.

Relevance to Your Research Interest

This is the single-most important factor at this stage of your search. Nothing else is remotely close. In fact, this is the only factor I recommend you use when you consider eliminating universities.

Is it possible for you to answer your research question at each university?

In order to answer this all-important question, you will need to look at the website for the university program to learn more about its contents. Remember in Step 1, I mentioned English program names at Japanese universities are not terribly descriptive. I also suggested that you add any program to your list that might be relevant to your research. Now, we will see whether they are.

Note about university websites in English

While most programs are going to have both Japanese and English websites, you will find that in many cases, the Japanese sites are far more detailed and thorough. If you have a friend who reads Japanese (preferably someone in your field of study) that you can ask for help as you review sites, you may get more information out of this step. Another option would be using a service like Google Translate to view the Japanese pages in translation, in addition to the English site. (If you cannot find the information you are searching for in English, that should be a red flag, but I'll cover that in the next section.)

I will include examples following the explanation, but for now, here are the steps that you're going to want to go through to evaluate each program.

Program overview

The first thing you want to look at is the program overview. In general, you are going to find quite a bit of meaningless fluff about programs' intentions to nurture future leaders for society, but you can ignore that. Your focus should be on the description of what fields the program teaches and where its emphasis is. Make sure that your research problem or question falls into one of those fields!

If the program description was particularly broad when you first created your list - for example, "Science and Engineering", you will want to pay particular attention to make sure that your sub-field is available and that it is taught in English!

Department/track/major names

I use all of these terms interchangeably. The specific terminology may vary from university to university, but each refers to smaller areas of focus within a graduate school. If the program has several different departments or majors, then your next step will be to look in more detail at the department, etc., that is most similar to your research question. After you decide which department is most appropriate for your research, add the department name to your list.

In general, you can only choose one department at any given university and your academic advisor must be from that department, too. If you think your research could fall into more than one department, then you should research both in more detail (see the steps below), and figure out which is the best choice for you.

Research centers

This will not always apply, but if a university has a named research center affiliated with your field of study, you can often find that information on the program website, as well. The presence of a research center that is affiliated with your particular research problem could be a strong benefit to you. It will typically mean that this is an area of emphasis for the university and that there will be more grant opportunities as well as more faculty and visiting researchers in your field.

Do not worry too much if there is no research center affiliated with your field of study, though. It is not common, so this is no reason to eliminate a university from your list.

Specific course offerings and syllabi

Not all university programs will list their course offerings or syllabi for those courses on their websites, but if they do, I recommend that you look through them! See what courses the program offers related to your field and what is covered in each course. Professors will typically teach courses related to their research focus areas, so the list of the courses should reflect the program's professors' areas of interest.

If you can, also find out which professors are responsible for each of the courses, as that can help you get started with the next step!

Professors' areas of specialization

The second half of your university-professor pair list is the name of the professor that you want to work with, and this is where we'll get started looking for candidates.

Many universities will have a list of the professors teaching in each department, including their research specialties or the courses they are responsible for. Take a close look at the professors and their fields to see how similar their research areas are to your own. If the professors have their own websites or pages, that can be a great place to find the subject of their most recent publications/presentations and current areas of research.

If there is not much information on the university website, you can also use Researchmap, which is the site we will use in the next chapter for the professor-first search. You can use Researchmap to search for faculty profiles at a particular university, which can help you find more details.

https://researchmap.jp/?lang=en

- On the page linked above, click "Researcher Search" in the top left then "Advanced Search" on the next page.
- In the "Affiliation" box, start typing the name of the university, and a list of matches should appear. Select the university name there.
- In the "Department" field, type the name of the graduate school or department that you find from the university website.
- Click search.

If you find a professor or professors that closely match your research interest, write their names in your list. At this point, it is not a problem to have multiple professors from the same university. Ultimately, you will only reach out to one professor at any particular university, but later in this chapter, we will go through a review of your potential advisors to help you choose the best one for your research. For now, you can leave every potential advisor on your list.

At this point, we are only looking for the professors' research interests to make sure there is at least one that matches your research question. We are not doing a full evaluation of how well-suited they are to supervise your research, so you do not need to scour their research profile in detail, yet. We will get to that later on in this chapter.

Rating

Once you have researched the program, department, and professors, it's time to assign a rating or value to each university. Of all the rankings you are going to conduct, this is one of the most important, by far. Here's how I recommend you rank your universities:

- Yes (circle): There is a department that matches your research interest as well as a professor with a specialization in the same field.
- Maybe (triangle): There is a department where your research could be included and some related courses, but not enough information to confirm if there is a matching professor or if your research field is a close enough match. A university should only be a "maybe" if there is not enough information to decide.
- No (X): There is no clear indication that your research topic could fit in the program or with any professor's research.

If a university is a "No" at this point, there is no point in continuing to research that university. The only consideration at this point in the search process is whether or not you can complete your research there.

If you are in the unfortunate position that you have to eliminate all of your universities, which should be quite rare if you have thought broadly about your research topic, then you would need to either reconsider your research topic and choose something possible in Japan, or reconsider whether the MEXT Scholarship and studying in Japan is really right for you.

I realize I have just thrown a lot of steps at you at once and you may be wondering how to apply them. In the next section, I'll go through a few examples of how to go through this evaluation process.

Examples

In this section, I am going to provide a few examples of how to evaluate the relevance of a program to your research interest. I have tried to include a variety of fields below, but I am obviously not an expert in all of them, so please pardon any errors or simplifications with regards to the actual research.

For the sake of simplicity, rather than complete research questions, I will refer just to the narrow field of research. The purpose here is to show the process. When you go through your search, you should already have a detailed research question in mind, so you would most likely be looking for even more specific details.

Please also note that when I refer to overall ratings for the universities below, it is in relation to my specific sample research topic, not the university or program as a whole. The programs that I have rejected below would still be excellent for other research fields!

Social sciences: Economics

For the purpose of this evaluation, my sample research question is about rural revitalization economics and my sample university is Tohoku University (the first one on JASSO's list). Here is the link to that program's top page, so that you can follow along:

https://www.econ.tohoku.ac.jp/english/page-graduate.html

Program overview

The website above indicates that the program includes education in economics and business administration as well as training in specialized fields such as accounting. It goes on to say that they have two major fields: 1. Economics and Management, and 2. Accounting. So far, my research question still fits within these fields.

Department/track/major names

My next step is to check the "Study Fields". The program has an extensive list of the fields they include at the link below:

https://www.econ.tohoku.ac.jp/english/page-study-field.html

From this list, my research topic would fall under "Practical Field > Regional Economic Policy Group > Regional Business Enterprises". So far, so good!

Research centers

The faculty has a "Regional Innovation Research Center", which sounds perfect for my research!

https://www.econ.tohoku.ac.jp/english/page-rirc.html

Specific course offerings and syllabi

Here's where the website falls short in English. The "Curriculum" page is even less detailed than the "Study Fields", so I would not be able to get any information there.

https://www.econ.tohoku.ac.jp/english/page-curriculum.html

However, this is also a great time to bring in a friend who speaks Japanese or get Google Translate going on the website, since the corresponding Japanese page shows all of the courses the program offers! Included in the Japanese list are courses in regional entrepreneurship, regional planning, development economics, agro-economics, etc., so I can be reasonably certain to find the coursework I need here related to my research. What's more, the professors that teach those courses could also be great targets for a future advisor!

https://www.econ.tohoku.ac.jp/econ/page-graduate-curriculum-curriculum01.html

Professors' areas of specialization

Tohoku has a list of all of the professors with their primary research field listed, which makes this search easy. There is one professor whose area of specialization is Regional Planning and another who specializes in Regional Enterprises. The latter would probably be my target professor, but I would write both on my list for future detailed evaluation.

https://www.econ.tohoku.ac.jp/english/page-teacher.html

Overall rating

Tohoku University's Graduate School of Economics and Management gets a definite "Yes" for my evaluation. Even if I had only been looking at the English pages and didn't find the list of courses, there is more than enough information here to be confident that I can explore my research topic in this program.

Social sciences (multidisciplinary): Japan studies

For the purposes of this example, my research question is about Japan's acceptance of non-traditional genders and my sample university is Saitama University. Saitama is the first university on JASSO's list under the category of "Cultural Studies" and has the promising program name, "Department of Japanese and Asia Studies".

Program overview

The program overview does not look promising for my research question. According to the website, the program's area of strengths are "Japanese military history and samurai culture, political and intellectual history, and the history and culture of performing arts."
http://hss.saitama-u.ac.jp/english/

Department/track/major names

From what I can tell, there is only one track within this program and students take courses in both "Japanese Culture" and "Asian Culture", though the latter only offers three courses. There is no information here that can help me tell if my research would fit.

Research centers

There are no research centers affiliated with my research field.

Specific course offerings and syllabi

There is a list in English of the courses offered, on the same page linked above. None of the courses mention gender studies in the title or descriptions, but there are a few courses that could approach the topic. "Edo Culture and the 'Bad Places'", which covers the history of the development of theater and prostitution districts, "Seminar in Contemporary Japanese Social Theory", and "Colloquium in Social Geography" all approach topics that could be peripheral to gender studies, if only because non-traditional genders in Japan are still considered to be unacceptable by many and could be lumped together with the topics covered in these programs. But this is ultimately a reach, with no clear information.

Professors' areas of specialization

Saitama has short profiles of all the professors who teach in the program, including their areas of specialty and publications. I started with the professor who teaches the "Seminar in Contemporary Japanese Social Theory", and "Colloquium in Social Geography" courses, but his research appears to focus on homelessness and urban revitalization. A search of the faculty profile page for the word "gender" also produces no hits. So, it does not look like there is a professor here that would be able to supervise my research topic.

http://hss.saitama-u.ac.jp/english/english_39.html

Overall rating

With no courses that explicitly cover gender studies and no professors that mention it in their profiles, Saitama gets a "No" for my research topic. I would cross it off my list (though I would not delete it - if I cannot find a target university at all and have to change my topic, I might come back to this in the future).

STEM: Materials science

For the purpose of this example, my research question is about fabricating new High Entropy Alloys (HEAs) for applications in transportation industry and my target university and program is Hokkaido University's "Division of Materials Science and Engineering". This isn't the first program on the list under Materials Engineering, but the first program is also at Hokkaido and is named the "Cooperative Program for Resources Engineering", so it does not seem as likely for my topic.

In general, for research in STEM fields you will need to find a professor with a very close match in their research field, since you will be associated with their lab and will often be assigned to work on a project contributing to the lab's overall goals. So, STEM applicants will have to be even more careful in their search than other fields.

Program overview

The program at Hokkaido, called the "English Engineering Education Program" covers a wide range of topics. In the brief program overview, one of the fields they mention is "material production methods", which sounds like it is related to my research topic in synthesizing new HEAs. https://www.eng.hokudai.ac.jp/e3/e3study/divisions/28-materials-scienc

<u>e-engineering</u>

Unfortunately, the bright orange button with a link to the Division's website is broken, at least as of the time of this writing.

Department/track/major names

Materials Science and Engineering is already the name of a division within the English Engineering Education Program. However, the division is further divided into four research groups, and there is a list of labs within each research group.

The research groups themselves do not have any description, and the titles (Ecological Materials, Materials Design, Energy Materials, and Energy Conversion Materials) are not sufficient to help me determine if my research topic will fit within them, but there are descriptions of the individual laboratories within each research group, which is even better.

. . . Except that none of them mention HEAs. There are a few that refer to alloys, but as far as I can tell from reading the information on this page, as well as the individual lab pages, they are focused on conventional alloys, so there are no labs where my research topic would obviously fit.

If I was an applicant searching, I would probably remove this program from my list at this point, but for the sake of the example, I will continue.

Research centers

I was not able to find any information about research centers on the division's website.

Specific course offerings and syllabi

I could not find any links to information about individual course offerings on the English site. However, I was able to find a syllabus search function on the Japanese website.
http://syllabus01.academic.hokudai.ac.jp/Syllabi/Public/Syllabus/SylList.aspx

The search function does allow you to narrow down course selections to courses taught in English, but you have to be able to read Japanese to use the search in the first place.

Regardless of that language issue, the search results returned no courses that mention HEAs in the course title, and when I read the syllabi of individual courses that mentioned materials, none referenced HEAs, so again, this looks like a dead end for my research.

Professors' areas of specialization

I mentioned the individual research labs' focuses above, and since the professors all belong to one of the labs, that information effectively covers their research areas.

One area where this program excels in providing information is that it has a list of past graduates' thesis abstracts.
https://www.eng.hokudai.ac.jp/e3/e3alumni/abstracts

The theses are grouped by year and division and are not searchable, but you would be able to browse through them to look for any that match your topics. Unfortunately, in the case of my sample research topic, I could not find any related theses, which is not surprising given the results of my research so far.

Overall rating

With no courses, labs, professors, or past theses that cover my research problem of High Entropy Alloys, Hokkaido gets a "No" for my research topic. I would cross it off my list.

Fine arts: Drawing

In fine arts, the goal of a degree program often is not research, but the creation of a portfolio or development of an exhibition of works. Despite this, applicants still need to fit in to the context and framework of the MEXT Scholarship application process. So, the "research output" would be replaced by the "exhibition of works" and the "research steps" would be acquiring the necessary skills to present that exhibition.

For the sake of this example, my "research problem" is to create an online exhibition of hand-drawn art, and my sample program is Tokyo University of the Arts' Global Art Practice, which is the only fine arts program on JASSO's list!

Program overview

The website does not have an overview page and the "About Curriculum" jumps directly to one of the subsections (and one that is not particularly descriptive of the curriculum). However, after checking the various pages on the site, I found that the "GAP (Global Arts Practice) Seminar" page introduces the first-year studies and the "Graduation Work and Research" page introduces the second year studies.

http://gap.geidai.ac.jp/corner83/cn9/gap_seminar_en.html
http://gap.geidai.ac.jp/corner83/cn9/graduationwork_en.html

From what I can tell, this program is very broad and responsive to students' individual art fields, so it looks like nearly all visual arts can be possible here. However, in the "GAP Seminar" page, there was a specific mention of a seminar in "Research and Practice of Drawing," so that is perfect for my topic.

Department/track/major names

There are no individual research tracks within the program.

Research centers

There are no research centers mentioned on the website.

Specific course offerings and syllabi

In this MFA program, there are no courses or credits. Students are enrolled in seminars throughout their studies and graduation is determined based on the quality of their graduation work or thesis.

Since I already confirmed that there was a seminar in drawing, this meets my needs!

Professors' areas of specialization

There is a faculty profiles section, but the professors' bios largely contain their feelings about art and nothing about their specializations, which is not helpful for my search.

However, the lecturers' profiles are more useful, and I found one specializes in drawing and also heads a group dedicated to "experimentation and research in drawing." That sounds perfect!

Overall rating

Fortunately, Tokyo University of the Arts gets a "Yes" for my evaluation. Since there were no other programs in the fine arts category on JASSO's list, this comes as a huge relief. (Although, if I was seeking to make a complete list here, I would also be looking through the uncategorized programs and other sections to see if there was anything else that might match my research interests, just in case this university did not work out.)

Quality of Information Available in English

In the preceding example section, I mentioned a few cases where programs had more information available in Japanese than they did in English. There was even one that had broken links on their English site, although they worked in Japanese.

What should this information mean to you and your search?

The quality of information about a program available in English can indicate how serious that program is about attracting international students. However, I would encourage you to look at this as a "positive" evaluation, rather than a "negative" one. What I mean is, do not look at a program website, conclude the information is lacking, and then decide that they must not be serious about attracting international students. It could just be that the university has a terrible website, in general.

This was my experience when I first looked at the Tokyo University of the Arts website in the example section. I thought the English information about the program was lacking and struggled to find details about courses and professors. But when I switched over to the Japanese site, I realized it was exactly the same. It's just not a great site in either language. The English is actually almost an exact match for the Japanese, and that shows me they are just as serious about bringing in international students as they are about students from Japan!

In the example sections, I also mentioned some universities that had a course list or course search system in Japanese, but not in English. But that doesn't necessarily mean that the specific program you're applying to isn't trying. Course search systems are generally university-wide and managed by the central IT department. Many rely on vendor software that can't handle multiple languages, so it's not something that the program can change, even if they want to.

What to look for

- Look for positives! For example, the Hokkaido University program that I mentioned in the examples had an extensive amount of information in English, including graduation theses of previous international students and an alumni database. That's more than you are going to find at many universities.
- Look for admission information. If the university is serious about attracting international students, then they are going to have admissions information for international students available in English. You will also be able to see if they require Japanese language ability from the admissions documents.(You might also find the information for MEXT Scholarship applicants in the admission information. If so, save that link for later reference!)
- Red flags. If the university does not have admissions information available in English or has only a brief description of the program, with no details, then there's a good chance that they are not particularly proactive about accepting international students. Even if they are willing to accept a MEXT scholar without Japanese language ability, consider that your study and research options might be limited there.

How to rate universities

For this criteria, remember that we are only looking at the quality of English language information available. So, I recommend you limit your rankings to "Yes" and "Maybe".

A "Yes" university is one that goes above and beyond, providing a higher level of detail than the others you research, for example details about past research, up-to-date news and events in English, etc.

A "Maybe" university is one that generally has enough information in English for you to make a decision about whether or not the program is right for you, and also has admissions information.

The only situation I would consider ranking a university "No" for this criteria is if you find a clear indication that Japanese language ability is mandatory for the program and you do not have the required level.

If a university is a "Yes" or "Maybe", certainly keep it on your list. If it is a "No" I would recommend moving it to the bottom of your priorities, or eliminating it if you have several better candidates.

Factors Related to Your Goals and Restraints

In the Preparation chapter, I encouraged you to know your goals from the outset. This section is where you will consider how those goals impact your university choice.

Remember that your relationship with your advisor is going to be the single-most important factor in the success of your studies. So, I would not recommend eliminating any universities from your list because of these goal factors. At most, they should serve as tie-breakers if you have two programs you are equally interested in.

Your goals are going to be unique to you, so do not feel the need to research any of these factors if you do not want to. I am just going to point out where you can find the information that I gave as examples in the earlier "Know Your Goals" section. Refer back to that section for how each of these factors might impact your experience, and decide which ones matter to you. Do not bother researching the factors below if they are not specific to your goals!

University and program size

You should be able to find this information on the university's website. Japanese universities are required to publicize this information, although they might only do it on their Japanese websites.

Often, you can find the total number of students at the university in the "About" section, or "In Numbers" page of the website. This should be further broken down into undergraduate and graduate students, as well as the number of students in each graduate school.

If the graduate school has its own pamphlet or brochure, that may also contain information about the number of students.

Note for University-Recommended MEXT Scholarship applicants:

If you are applying for the University-Recommended MEXT Scholarship, then it is valuable to know how many international graduate students the university has, since that will impact the number of slots they have for MEXT Scholarships. Unfortunately, it is not always possible to find this information, since universities are not required to publish that level of detail. However, English-language pamphlets will often include those numbers, since they want to appeal to future students!

Location

Every university's website should have its address listed, either at the bottom of the page or on an "Access" page. Take that address and plug it into your favorite map website or app to get an idea of there the university is within Japan. You can also Google the city name to learn more about the location, such as its environment, cost of living, etc.

University ranking

The most well-known ranking sites that cover Japanese universities are Times Higher Education (THE) and Quacquarelli Symonds (QS). THE also has a specific ranking of Japanese universities that uses a different set of criteria from the international ranking. Consider the factors that go into each ranking before you use them as a data point in your decision.

In general, the best way I have found to find ranking information is to simply Google the name of the university with "ranking" at the end. You can also add the name of the ranking you are interested in (QS, Times Higher Education, etc.) and/or the name of specific graduate school where you want to study, as well.

How to rate these factors

In your university research table (you can use the spreadsheet in the bonus download materials), add a column for each of the goal factors that you plan to evaluate. I do not recommend a Yes/Maybe/No rating for these factors. Instead, enter the exact data you find. So, for size, write down the number of students, etc. That will be a better reference for you later on as you compare your programs.

Remember that your relationship with your academic advisor should be the most important factor in your search. Try not to get too worried or focused on these factors now and let that impression cloud your interaction with professors later.

Relationship Factors

One last factor you'll want to consider regarding your target universities is relationships. The old saying, "It's not what you know, it's *who* you know that matters" is true in academia and relationships are particularly important in Japan. A simple introduction by a common acquaintance can earn you a more careful evaluation. It will not necessarily guarantee admission, or anything like that, but it should guarantee that your application gets attention and therefore has the chance to stand on its merits.

There are a few kinds of relationships to consider:

Official university partnerships

I mentioned this earlier in the process of creating your list of universities, but if you haven't looked up whether there are any partnerships between your university and universities on your target list, now is the time to do so! As I mentioned in the earlier step, mark any partner university on your list with a star.

If you are applying for the University-Recommended MEXT Scholarship, these partner universities should be the first ones that you consider. If you are applying for the Embassy-Recommended MEXT Scholarship, they should still be high on your list because of the potential for personal connections.

Personal connections

Chances are good that you do not know anyone at your target universities personally, particularly not in the faculty or staff. However, if you do, that is a great place to start! For example, if you have been actively working on your Japan network by attending functions and events held by the Japanese embassy and making connections there, there is a possibility that some of the people you met could be related to universities in Japan. But that is a rare situation, so do not be discouraged if you do not have any direct connections yet.

More common are second- or third-degree connections. Maybe you know someone who knows someone at a university in Japan. For example, it is common for former MEXT Scholars to be asked to give presentations once they return to their home countries. If you meet one of those MEXT alumni and they still have contacts at their old university, that is a personal connection you might be able to use.

Note: I do not recommend that you contact them just yet. We are not ready to start reaching out to universities. For now, just note that relationship on the list of universities.

Other types of personal relationships can be former students from your current university who are currently MEXT scholars, or simply studying abroad in Japan. Even if you do not know them personally, if you have a way to get in touch with them, such as through your university international office or their former advisor, that's potentially a connection you can leverage.

Direct relationships between faculty members at your university and your target university can also be an opportunity for an introduction.

Ultimately, with personal relationships, your goal is to identify someone who can put in a good word for you with your target advisor in Japan. It can be as simple as "I know a student at X university who is really interested in your work and wants to study under you in the future. Is it alright if I put her in touch with you?" Even something that simple is likely to get you more attention and consideration than a cold email would.

If you can identify a potential personal connection at any of the universities in Japan on your list, go ahead and mark that with a star, as well (or an additional star if you have both a personal relationship and a partnership!)

STEP 3: IDENTIFY PROFESSORS

The last step of evaluating your universities is to find a potential faculty advisor at each one who can supervise your research. After all, the goal here is to create a list of university-professor pairs.

You want to identify one first-choice professor at each university. I often get asked if it is OK to contact two professors at the same university as potential supervisors. My answer is always no, not at the same time. It is well and good to have a back-up professor at a university, in case your first choice professor proves unable to supervise you, but you should only ever be trying to contact one at a time, so it is important to prioritize. If you cannot choose between two professors to determine which would be best to supervise you, then I would argue that you haven't yet done enough research about them.

So, what does that research look like? How should you go about evaluating your professor? Here's how to start.

I have also included a professor profile spreadsheet in the bonus documents for this chapter.

The university/program website

Often, universities will have a faculty database that introduces each professor's area of research, possibly including the courses they teach. This is a great place to look up professors' areas of interest to make sure that it intersects with your own research.

Earlier in this chapter, when evaluating programs, I talked about looking for professors who have matching research fields, teach related courses, or have labs related to your research. If you can find any of those on the university website, that's a great start!

A note about professor ranks: Applicants often ask me if their advisor must be a full professor, or if they can have an associate or assistant professor as an advisor. It depends on the university, so you will have to check with them directly to find out. For now, I would recommend that you do not eliminate any professors from your list of potential advisors because of their ranks. Even if they cannot be your academic supervisor, their superior likely could be your official supervisor, giving you the opportunity to work with them.

However, I would recommend that you be wary about Visiting Professors, or any other title that shows that the person is not a full-time staff member at the university. You will need an academic advisor who will remain at the university throughout your degree, so you should avoid someone who is likely to leave.

Professors' personal websites

It isn't uncommon for faculty members to have their own websites, or websites for their labs. These sites might be part of their universities' websites, or they might be independent. Sometimes you will find them linked from the university website, but another way to find them is a to search Google for the professor's name. Add the university or program name, too, for the sake of clarification.

If you find a professor has their own website with information about their ongoing research, especially if it is in English and up-to-date, that is a strong sign that the professor is active in their research and proactive about international collaboration, which are both excellent signs that they may be a good target as a future advisor.

If the professor doesn't have their own website, or at least an active profile on a website or database, it could indicate the reverse - that they are not proactive about their research or international collaboration.

Researchmap

Researchmap is the website I recommend using if you are searching by professor first, instead of university first, but it is also useful to evaluate potential advisors within a program. You can use Researchmap if the university website doesn't offer detailed information about individual professors (or doesn't have that information in English) or once you have the name of a target professor and want to learn more about their research interests and activity level.

https://researchmap.jp/?lang=en

Access the URL above, and click "Researcher Search" in the header, then click "Advanced Search" on the next page.

If you have the name of the professor you want to look up, you can enter that in the "name" field and hit search right away.

If you do not have a name yet, start typing the name of the university in the

"Affiliation" field. It should start suggesting universities, so once you find the one you are looking for in that list, click on it.

Unfortunately, the "Department" field is not so accommodating. As of the time I tested the site in February 2021, "Department" allows you to search in English, but only shows suggestions in Japanese. You can still type the name of the graduate school in English and use that to search for a list of faculty members associated with that graduate school.

Once you have your search results, you can click on the individual professors' profiles to see their research interests, where and when they earned their degrees and where they have taught, as well as lists of publications, presentations, and awards. In the next section, I will go into more detail on what parts of their profile to focus on and how to interpret the information you find there.

If a professor does not have a Researchmap profile, but you find their personal website or lab website, you can look for the same information there, as well!

Advanced Research on Your Professors

Not every professor is going to have an active Researchmap profile or their own website, so it may be harder to find this information for some of the potential advisors that you try to research. In that case, the lack of a profile or website itself is also an important factor to consider.

Having a personal website, lab website, or Researchmap profile is essentially a requirement for any researcher who is interested in collaborating internationally or playing an active role in their field. It serves as a constantly accessible CV and a home base for communicating with colleagues around the world. If you find that a professor you are trying to research does not

have an accessible profile or website, think hard about what that says about
the professor. Unless they're famous enough that everyone knows them and
they don't need to bother with a profile (unlikely), it is almost certainly a
sign that they are not proactive or interested in international collaboration.

For the rest of this section, I'm going to assume that you have identified a
professor who has a Researchmap profile or detailed website. I'll be referring
to the sections of the Researchmap profile, since it's the most common
organization system you'll find, but you should be able to find much of the
same information on a personal site, as well.

Here are some items to look for:

Affiliation

All professors have a "home" affiliation in a particular college, faculty, or
graduate school. You want to make sure the professors you are looking
up are affiliated with the *graduate school* you want to apply to, not just the
corresponding undergraduate college. Professors can be affiliated with both.
A professor must be affiliated with the graduate school in order to supervise
graduate students!

Research interest

If the professor describes their current research interest fields, make sure
that matches with what you want to study. Of course, you can get much
more detailed information by looking up their recent publications!

Activity level (publications, etc.)

You should be able to find a list of your potential advisor's recent publications, presentations, and awards. In particular, look for how often that professor publishes or presents in English. What constitutes "frequent" or "regular" publications may vary from field to field, but if you notice it has been years - or decades - since the professor has presented or published anything new, that should be a red flag that he or she is not active in the field.

Other resources for activity levels

Another resource to check researchers' activity levels and relevance is Google Scholar.
https://scholar.google.com/

Searching for a professor's name on that site will pull up a list of any recent publications within the journals that Google Scholar uses. If the person also has a profile on the site, you can see a list of all their articles and organize them by the number of times others have cited them. There is also a handy graph that shows the number of publications by year.

If the faculty member you are researching is publishing in English in well-known journals in your field (if you don't know which ones are well known, ask your current academic advisor), then that's an excellent sign. But if the professor is publishing in Japanese, and therefore not in international journals, that's not always a bad thing, as long as they are active.

Google Scholar does not cover every journal, so another resource you can use to check your target advisor's recent activity is your university library! Do an author search for the professor in e-journal databases to see where and how often they publish.

Don't forget to bookmark or save links to the articles you find by any professor you are interested in. You'll want to read as many of them as possible before contacting the professor later.

Age (years since bachelor's degree)

I am not being ageist, this is actually an important factor. Japan has a mandatory retirement age, so you need to be concerned about your potential advisor's age to make sure they aren't planning to retire in the middle of your degree!

As I write this in 2021, Japan's universities are in the middle of a significant wave of faculty retirements. Over this last year, I had more applicants than ever before contact me to say that their applications for Letters of Acceptance were rejected because their target advisor was planning to retire and there was nobody else who could supervise their research. A faculty friend also confirmed this is a trend.

At many universities in Japan, the mandatory retirement age for faculty and staff members is 60 or 65, as of 2021. Keeping in mind that Japanese often go straight from high school into university (or, at least, that would have been the norm when current professors were students), that means that they may retire 38 years after earning their bachelor's degree. As a rule of thumb, I recommend that you be very cautious about targeting potential advisors who earned their bachelors' degrees 30 years ago or more.

Seniority

This relates to age, but beyond looking at whether the professor is a risk to retire soon, you need to think about what your advisor's career level might mean for your relationship to them. Here are some general pros and cons to consider. Of course, each individual is going to be different, but these trends are common.

Young/early career

What does every junior faculty want? Tenure and advancement. The way they get there is by being active in the field, academic achievements, and taking the lead in new areas. For Japanese universities, those "new areas" often include internationalization.

So an early career advisor is likely to be more active in their research and proactive in their labs. They are also likely to be up-to-date on the field and on technology - even something as simple as websites. In Japan, in particular, there also seems to be a trend that the younger professors are better at English and work with more international programs.

On the negative side, they will have less experience as a supervisor and will probably have less access to funding. You might also encounter a junior professor that is so passionate about their own advancement that they do not have time for their advisees. They won't have as large of a network for collaboration and job placements as others, if that is important to you, though they might still be connected to their own former advisor's network.

Senior faculty

Senior faculty members have longer track records and there's a better chance they are a known name in the field. They will be experienced and are likely to have access to more funding, plus a stronger voice in the university's decision-making process. If you're looking for faculty help with job placement after graduation, senior professors are likely to have the largest network of former advisees and colleagues around the field.

The downside to a senior faculty member is that they no longer have the pressure to perform, so they may be less active - particularly if they are close to retirement. Sometimes, they may hold additional responsibilities or titles that take away time they have to spend with advisees. They can be set in their ways and not as willing to work with fresh ideas. They are also the least likely to be familiar with recent technology or proficient in English.

Mid-career

Mid-career faculty members combine the positives and negatives of the earlier categories. They will be a little more established than a junior faculty member and have earned some recognition within the field. But they're not at the top and will still be seeking further advancement, so there will be pressure on them to remain active.

In terms of negatives, they combine lesser degrees of the other two groups. Mid-career faculty members might be at a higher risk of taking a sabbatical than either of the other groups, but there is no way that you can tell that in advance.

Advisees

You won't be able to find information about students that professor has advised in the past on Researchmap, but you may find it on their lab website, personal website, or university website.

If you can find information about current or past advisees, try to find out what their thesis or dissertation topics were and compare them to your own topic. If the professor has supervised similar thesis topics to what you want to research, that is a good sign that they will be a fit for your studies, as well.

STEP 4: PRIORITIZING YOUR UNIVERSITY-PROFESSOR PAIRS

Hopefully, by following the tips above, you now have a clear picture of each of your potential advisors' current research interests, activities, and suitability to supervise your research. As I mentioned at the start of this section, once you have done enough research on each professor, there should be only one "best" professor to supervise your research at any university, as well as overall.

At this point, I recommend you start a new list - yes, another one. In this list, you are going to be grouping university-professor pairs.

As you fill in this list, prioritize the pairs *based on the professor*. Remember, the most important factor in the success of your studies in Japan is your relationship with your advisor. Finding the best advisor should be more important than any of the criteria that you looked up about the universities, though the university details can be a tie-breaker, if needed.

If you are planning to apply for the Embassy-Recommended MEXT Scholarship, you'll need a list of three universities and professors for your application. If you're applying for the University-Recommended MEXT Scholarship, you can only apply to one university and one supervisor there. However, in either case, you'll want to have more targets than that for now.

In the second half of this book, I will walk you through getting into contact with your potential supervisors in Japan. During that step, you may find that professors are unresponsive or that they are unwilling or unable to supervise your research. If that happens, you will need to have alternatives.

So, when you make your list, do not stop at one or three names. Keep going and prioritize all the potential supervisors and universities that you have identified so far.

Keep in mind, too, that you should only ever be in touch with one professor at any university at a time. If you have multiple professors that you are interested in working with at one university, even if they are in different graduate schools, choose the one best fit. You will only be able to reach out to the others if that first-choice professor does not work out.

PROGRESS CHECK

You should have a list of target university-professor pairs for your MEXT Scholarship application, ranked in priority order. Congratulations! It has taken a lot of work to get to this point.

You are halfway done with this book. But, if you are contacting professors in advance, then before you move on to actually reaching out to them, it's time to shift gears and go back to your academic research. If you have already submitted your Field of Study and Research Program Plan to the embassy, or it is too late to change it, then you can skip ahead to Chapter 4: How to Make Initial Contact.

If you haven't yet done so, your next step is to write your Field of Study and Research Program Plan, *targeting it at your first-choice professor*. When we started this book, you should have had your research question, or at least a research problem. Now, look at it again and make sure it is similar enough to your target advisor's research. If not, think about what you can do to make it closer, so that your advisor will not only be able to supervise your research but also be excited to have you as their advisee.

With that knowledge and focus in mind, finish writing or polishing your Field of Study and Research Program Plan.

If you need to know more about how to write your Field of Study and Research Program Plan, I have a few articles about the format on my website, and the second book in this *Mastering the MEXT Scholarship Series* will walk you through the process of writing it, from idea to finished proposal. You can find more information at the links below:

Book: How to Write a Scholarship-Winning Field of Study and Research Program Plan

https://www.transenzjapan.com/blog/mastering-the-mext-scholarship/how-to-write-a-scholarship-winning-field-of-study-and-research-program-plan/

Article: "Field of Study and Research Program Plan: 2019-2020 MEXT Scholarship - Updated"

*This article covers the new format for the Field of Study and Research Program Plan introduced in 2019 for the Embassy-Recommended MEXT Scholarship.
https://www.transenzjapan.com/blog/field-of-study-and-research-program-plan-2019-2020-mext-scholarship-updated/

Article: "MEXT Scholarship Field of Study and Research Program Plan Elements"

*This article covers the "old" format of the Field of Study and Research Program Plan, which is still being used for the University-Recommended MEXT Scholarship, as of the 2020-2021 application cycle.
https://www.transenzjapan.com/blog/mext-scholarship-field-of-study-and-research-program-plan-elements/

What to do next

You can skip the next chapter of this book, "How to Create Your Universit y-Professor List: Starting with Professors". That chapter covers another method to arrive at the same list of professors and universities that you have already created, so you do not need to go through that process again.

Once you have finished your Field of Study and Research Program Plan and gotten it to where you are comfortable showing it to a potential future advisor in Japan, skip ahead to the chapter on "How to Make Initial Contact".

EXERCISES

I highly recommend that you download the free exercise worksheets I have created, especially for this chapter. These bonus worksheets include template spreadsheets for all the lists I have described.

https://www.transenzjapan.com/mext/uniprofexercises

Basics

1. What level of degree are you applying for in Japan?

2. What field of study are you interested in applying for?

3. List at least five different ways to describe your field of study, including broader descriptions of the field and alternative ways of describing it.

University list

4. Using the websites described in this chapter, list every university and program that could include your research field. (I recommend using the downloadable spreadsheet from the bonus documents or creating your own spreadsheet for this, since you will add information to these universities as you go further with your research!)

- University Name
- Program Name
- Program Language
- Program Level
- Website

Partner university list

5. Add any partner universities in Japan to your list, including the same information as in the University List, above.

   *If the partner university is already in your University List, above, mark it with a star - you'll want to research those first!

Adding details - research relevance

In your list, add columns for the following topics.

6. Department/Track/Major Name: Only include the one that your research topic would fall under, if appropriate.

7. Research Center: Fill in the name of any research centers related to your field of study, if applicable.

8. Relevant Courses: List any course names that apply to your research topic.

9. Instructor: For each of the courses in 8, list the name of the instructor.

10. Other Relevant Professors: Fill in the names of any other professors that might be related to your research field.

11. Program Relevance Rating: As explained in Step 2, rank the program's relevance to your research interest on a "Yes/Maybe/No" scale. For any "No", you can cross them off your list (or hide the row, if you are working with the template spreadsheets). You will not need to research them any further.

Adding details - goal relevance

Only add and research the following columns if you have already decided that they are important to your research and graduation goals. Refer to questions 4-7 in the Chapter 1 Exercise and only look up those items.

12. Size (Optional): Fill in the number of students for the university and for the graduate school, including the number of international students.

13. Location (Optional): Fill in the city where the university is located.

14. Rank (Optional): Fill in the university's ranking - be sure to use the same ranking system for all universities, if available. You can't compare rankings between systems!

15. Goal Relevance Rating: If you filled in any of the columns above, give each university a ranking on the "Yes/Maybe/No" scale. However, unlike the Research Relevance ranking above, I do not recommend that you eliminate any universities from your list based on a "No" here, unless it truly is a deal breaker and you would rather have no MEXT Scholarship at all, rather than

studying there!

Relationships

You should have already starred any universities where you have an official partnership, so this is for unofficial partnerships.

16. Mark any university where you have a personal relationship or a potential personal relationship with a star - or a second star, if you also have an official partnership.

17. Fill in the name and contact information of your connection with that university.

Professor profile

18. Create a new list for professors, or use the spreadsheet in the bonus worksheets, and fill in the information below for each potential advisor you are interested in at each of the universities remaining on your list.

- Name
- Rank (Professor, Associate Professor, Assistant Professor, Lecturer, etc.)
- Sex
- Department
- Area of research interest
- Courses taught
- Lab name/website (if applicable)
- Any international faculty/students in lab? (yes/no)
- Personal website (if applicable)
- Most recent publication title, date, and language
- Most recent presentation title, date, and language

- Common subject themes in recent publications/presentations
- Most recent update to personal website/lab website/researchmap profile
- Date earned bachelor's degree
- Estimated date of retirement ((date of bachelor's degree)+38 years)
- Email/phone number (if possible)

The final university-professor pair list

19. Make one final list of the remaining universities and one first-choice professor at each, including the information below:

- University Name
- Graduate School Name
- Professor Name
- Program Website
- MEXT Scholarship Application Information Page
- Professor's Contact Information

CHAPTER THREE: HOW TO SEARCH BY PROFESSOR

In the last chapter, I covered one method to create your list of university-professor pairs, starting with the university. In this chapter, I will go into the second method. Both chapters describe different ways to reach the same goal. So, if you already have a list from the previous chapter, you can skip this one and move on to Chapter 4: How to Make Initial Contact.

Of course, if you're still trying to decide which method is best for you, or the university-first method did not meet your needs, read on!

Where you should be

Before you look up potential advisors in Japan, you need to be very clear about what you want to research in Japan and why. This knowledge is important for the professor-first search method. This search method focuses on the similarity between your research interests and your potential advisor's, so if you don't have your research question clear in your mind, you will have no basis to search and compare.

For the university-first search method, I said that you should at least have a research problem in mind before looking up programs. But the professor-first search is most appropriate for applicants who already have a research question. If your own research goals are unclear, you may find that this method leads to a frustrating dead end or confusion. In that case, I recommend the university-first approach.

If you're clear on your research and ready to move on, keep reading!

OVERVIEW OF SEARCHING BY PROFESSOR

Just like I did in the last chapter, I want to start by describing the process of searching by professor and who it might work best for.

In this process, your first step will be to create a list of all the faculty members in Japan who could supervise your research.

Once you have that list, you will analyze the potential supervisors to determine which ones might be best. I will introduce a few sources for that analysis as well as what you should look for, at a minimum.

Your third step will be to study the potential advisors' universities and programs. In this step, you will make sure that each potential advisor teaches in a degree program in English. However, even if they don't, I will suggest a way that you may still work with them.

Finally, you will look at all the data you have collected and rank your potential advisors.

By the end of this process, just like the university-first method, you will have a list of professors who are affiliated with programs taught in English, prioritized by their suitability to supervise your research topic.

Benefits of this approach

This approach is best if you have a strong research interest and do not want to deviate from it. Since you will start your list based on professors with similar research interests, you can more confident of a strong connection with them in the end. Unlike the university-first approach, where you start with a program name, you will avoid the trap of finding an interesting program only to learn that there are no professors there who can supervise your research.

Another benefit is that this method helps you collect information about your potential advisor that you will need anyway before you reach out to contact him or her. You'll also have extensive information about other faculty members in the field across Japan, which can help later with collaborations and building your academic network within the country. All the research you conduct into potential advisors can be beneficial to you later.

This approach might also help you identify connections that would not be possible with the university-first method. During this search process, you will most likely come across faculty members with a common research interest, but who do not teach in an English-language program. However, I will introduce a way that you may still work with them either formally or informally, which can help advance your research goals.

The professor-first method is also best for fields where you need a strong research connection, such as STEM fields where you will be part of a professor's lab and your research must fit within the lab's area of interest.

These are the primary benefits of the professor-first search. Of course, there are some drawbacks, as well. Consider both before deciding whether this approach or the university-first search is best for you.

Limitations of this approach

This method can lead to some frustrating dead ends. In the "benefits" section, above, I mentioned a way that you might work with researchers in your field even if they are not affiliated with a program taught in English. However, they wouldn't be able to be your primary advisor in that situation, and that method will only work sometimes, when there is a similar enough English-taught program. So, you could find yourself in a situation where you find a potential advisor that you are excited to work with, only to learn that it won't be possible.

The method is less methodical than searching for universities first, so there is a possibility of missing some opportunities. With the university-first search, you start with a broad definition of your field and narrow down to your research interest, so you have a better chance of identifying every possible program. However, when you start with your narrow field of interest, you will use specific terminology. If you are not careful to explore similar wording or alternative ways of describing your research, you could miss out on finding an opportunity because you used a different keyword for your search.

As I have mentioned a few times already, this search method is not useful if you do not already have a clear idea of what you want to research. If you only have a general field or issue that you want to explore, you can end up with a list of potential supervisors with varying topics, making it hard to make your final decision.

Which method will you choose?

If after reading the pros and cons above, you want to move forward with the professor-first search, read on! Otherwise, consider skipping back a chapter to the university-first search for a more methodical approach.

Over the rest of this chapter, I will go through each of the steps in the search process in more detail and there will be an exercise section at the end of the chapter, as well as spreadsheet templates in the downloadable bonus documents, that will help you keep track of your progress as you go.

Regardless of your search method, remember that, for now, your first goal should be to create as extensive of a list as possible. Once you contact potential supervisors, later in this book, you might find they are not available or that they do not meet your needs, so you'll want to have more options than necessary to make sure that you have a backup plan in place.

STEP 1: CREATE YOUR LIST OF PROFESSORS

The first step in creating your list of university-professor pairs is to identify as many potential advisors as possible in Japan. In this first step, we will cast a wide net to add names to that list.

For now, focus on adding. Treat this like a brainstorming stage and do not start eliminating advisors just yet.

I will introduce four methods below for identifying potential supervisors in Japan, most of which are available to anybody, anywhere. Of course, these methods are not exhaustive, so please use any other resources you can find.

During this first step, I recommend you record at least the following information for each potential V you find. You can use the bonus worksheets associated with this chapter to help you keep track.

- Name
- Research focus area
- Name of university and graduate school
- Link to personal profile

For that last one, I recommend recording where you found the professor's information. We will come back later to examine each potential supervisor in more detail.

Names from Previous Research

The first place to find names from is your previous research.

Since you are searching by professor, I assume that you already have a clear research question that you have created after conducting a literature review related to your field of study.

If you haven't already, go through the works you used for your literature review to check if any of the authors are affiliated with Japanese universities. For the author of the work itself, you can usually find this information within the book or article.

I also recommend that you go through the bibliography or citations of the works you reviewed. Pick out the citations that were most related to your research interest or any sources that refer to Japan and research those authors to find out if any of them are in Japan. In most cases, a Google search for the author can help you find that information.

You should also go through any other works in your field that you have read in the past, such as for research papers in your previous degree, and do the same thing.

One quick note here: Don't assume a professor is Japanese or affiliated with a Japanese university just because they have a Japanese name. Conversely, don't assume that a professor with a non-Japanese name is not affiliated with a Japanese university - especially if they have written about Japan or used examples in Japan in the past!

Researchmap

https://researchmap.jp/?lang=en

If you do not have any potential advisor names from your previous research, then the first place I recommend looking for new names is through the website Researchmap, because it focuses on Japan and is quite comprehensive. If you read through the previous chapter, you will remember that I introduced this site for follow-up research once you had a list of names or a university program, but you can also use it to find potential supervisors by field of study, as well.

Researchmap is a site operated by the Japanese Science and Technology Agency, which is an official government body. It collects data on researchers and research institutions and also allows researchers to create their own profiles on the site. When you first visit the site, it may default to Japanese unless you use the language code in the link above, but you can change the language in the top right corner.

Most important to you, it has a robust search tool you can use to identify potential future advisors.

Researcher search

The best way to use this site is the "Researcher Search" function in the header. There is also a "Community Search" but you have to be a registered member of the site in order to view any of the contents in the various community pages, so that is not as useful to you.

To use the Researcher Search function, click that link, then the link for "Advanced Search", which will give you several options you can use.

Department field

I recommend you start with either the "Department" field, where you can enter free text, or the "Field" and "Subfield" boxes. The "Research Interests" field search is not particularly powerful, and could return misleading results. For example, I typed in several variations of "Japanese History" and got no results for any of them. However, when I found researchers in Japanese history using the "Subfield" box (History - Japan), there was a long list, and several of them even had "Japanese History" listed as a research interest on their profile.

If you use the Department search, be sure to try a few different variations on your field of study, from narrow to broad search terms. You should also try single words rather than multi-word phrases. This search appears to function as a pattern match. It will only return results if the term that you entered in the search box appears in that exact order in the individual professor's profile.

To give an example of what I mean, "Aerospace" returned 170 results, but "Aerospace engineering" returned only 114, because of universities that did not use the name in that exact order. The search term "Aeronautical" returned only 29 results.

Field and subfield

Using the "Field" and "Subfield" boxes allows you to browse through a list of search terms, which saves you from having to think about what term would be best to use. The "Field" box will limit the options that appear in the

"Subfield" box, so start there. The "Subfield" box is not in alphabetical order (or any other discernible order), so be sure to look through each option.

Links to related professors

Once you have run a search and start browsing through individual profiles, you can use some sections of those profiles to help you find additional potential advisors, as well. The "Research Interests" and "Research Areas" are clickable links that you can use to find other professors with a similar interest. You can also find links to coauthors that each researcher has worked with. If you find any new potential advisors through those links, add them to your list!

Beware of research rabbit holes

There is a lot of data on this site, and it can be easy to get caught up in reading all of it. But for now, try to avoid that temptation. We will come back to review it later, when we analyze all the names on your list. For now, just record the information I described above, save the link, and move on.

Additional Research Resources

If you have gone through the Researchmap search, you should have identified most relevant researchers in your field in Japan. However, since search terms can be fickle and not all researchers will keep an active profile on that site, it is useful to follow up with a few additional searches to make sure that nobody has slipped past your notice.

Journals and e-journals

If you have access to journals or e-journals in your field of study, such as through your university library, that is a great resource to find researchers who are actively publishing in your field. Scan through the last year of articles in each relevant journal and look up the authors for any that are similar to your research interest to find out if they are affiliated with Japanese universities.

Google

You can also search Google for keywords related to your field of study along with "university Japan". Scour the search results for academic articles, references to publications, presentations, conferences, or news articles and fill out your list of potential advisors with any promising leads that come up.

This can also be a good way to find contact information for professors who are otherwise difficult to get in touch with. I have often been able to find professors' email addresses from a CV or bio posted on an old, forgotten conference website, even when it wasn't available via the professor's university. If you find their contact information, keep track of it for later!

Use Your Network

Your network starts with your current and/or former academic advisors, but you should also consider anyone you know who studied or worked in Japan, particularly if they are related to your research field.

Ask your academic advisor or other contacts if they know of anyone doing research in your field in Japan. Of course, let them know you are doing your own research as well! If they suggest any names, do your homework to look up more about those potential advisors to make sure they are close enough to your research topic.

If reaching out through your network yields an offer for an introduction, that's a great bonus, but I would caution you against jumping on it too soon. Ideally, you want to be prepared before you get into direct contact with potential supervisors in Japan, and that means having your Field of Study and Research Program Plan ready to show them, if requested.

I also recommend that you go through the next step, advanced research, at a minimum before accepting an introduction offer.

STEP 2: ADVANCED RESEARCH ON YOUR PROFESSORS

Now that you have a list of names along with research fields, it's time to dig into the details. You'll be going back to Researchmap, even for faculty members that you found through other approaches, and also searching to see if the potential advisors on your list have personal websites or lab websites.

As I pointed out in the previous chapter, whether your potential advisor even has a Researchmap profile or personal/lab website is an important piece of information for you to consider. Any researcher who is interested in international collaboration will need to have some kind of "home base" that advertises their research activities to the international community. If you find a professor that has no online profile, that is almost certainly a sign that they are not proactive or interested in international collaboration.

If you read through the "Advanced Research on Your Professor" section in the previous chapter, this is mostly going to be a repetition, but I assume that most readers will choose only one of the two chapters to read and follow.

For the rest of this section, I'm going to assume that you have identified a professor who has a Researchmap profile or detailed website. I'll be referring to the sections of the Researchmap profile, since it's the most common organization system you'll find, but you may find the same information on a personal site, as well. As you research, add this information to your table of potential advisors for easy reference and comparison later.

Here are some items to look for:

Affiliation

All professors have a "home" affiliation in a particular college, faculty, or graduate school. You want to make sure the professors you are looking up are affiliated with the *graduate school* you want to apply to, not just the corresponding undergraduate college. There is a chance that professors can be affiliated with both. A professor must be affiliated with the graduate school in order to supervise graduate students!

Research interest

You should have already written this down in the previous step, but just in case, if the professor describes their current research interest fields, make sure that matches with what you want to study. Of course, you can get much more detailed information by looking up their recent publications!

Activity level (publications, etc.)

You should be able to find a list of your potential advisor's recent publications, presentations, and awards. In particular, look for how often that professor publishes or presents in English. What constitutes "frequent" or "regular" publications may vary from field to field, but if you notice it has been years - or decades - since the professor has presented or published anything new, that should be a red flag that he or she is not active in the field.

Other resources for activity levels

Another resource to check researchers' activity levels and relevance is Google Scholar.
https://scholar.google.com/

Searching for a professor's name on that site will pull up a list of any recent publications they are affiliated with within the journals that Google Scholar uses. If the person also has a profile on the site, you can see a list of all their articles and organize them by the number of times they have been cited by others. There is also a handy graph that shows the number of publications by year.

If the faculty member you are researching is publishing regularly in English in well-known journals in your field (if you don't know which ones are well known, ask your current academic advisor), then that's an excellent sign. But if the professor is publishing primarily in Japanese, and therefore not in international journals, that's not necessarily a bad thing, as long as they are active.

Google Scholar does not cover every journal, so another resource you can use to check your target advisor's recent activity is your university library! Do an author search for the professor in e-journal databases to see where and how often they publish.

Don't forget to bookmark or save links to the articles you find by any professor you are interested in. You'll want to read as many of them as possible before contacting the professor later.

Age (years since bachelor's degree)

I am not being ageist, this is actually an important factor. Japan has a mandatory retirement age, so you need to be concerned about your potential advisor's age to make sure they aren't planning to retire in the middle of your degree!

As I write this in 2021, Japan's universities are in the middle of a significant wave of faculty retirements. Over this last year, I had more applicants than ever before contact me to say that their applications for Letters of Acceptance were rejected because their target advisor was planning to retire and there was nobody else who could supervise their research. A faculty friend also confirmed this is a trend.

At many universities in Japan, the mandatory retirement age for faculty and staff members is 60 or 65, as of 2021. Keeping in mind that Japanese tend to go straight from high school into university (or, at least, that would have been the norm when current professors were students), that means that they may retire 38 years after earning their bachelor's degree. As a rule of thumb, I would recommend that you be very cautious about targeting potential advisors who earned their bachelors' degrees 30 years ago or more.

Seniority

This relates to age, but beyond looking at whether the professor is a risk to retire soon, you need to think about what your advisor's career level might mean for your relationship to them. Here are some general pros and cons to consider. Of course, each individual is going to be different, but these trends are fairly common.

Young/early career

What does every junior faculty want? Tenure and advancement. The way they get there is by being active in the field, academic achievements, and taking the lead in new areas. For Japanese universities, those "new areas" often include internationalization.

So an early career advisor is likely to be more active in their research and proactive in their labs. They are also likely to be up-to-date on the field and on technology - even something as simple as websites. In Japan, in particular, there also seems to be a trend that the younger professors are better at English and work with more international programs.

On the negative side, they will have less experience as a supervisor and will probably have less access to funding. You might also encounter a junior professor that is so passionate about their own advancement that they do not have time for their advisees. They won't have as large of a network for collaboration and job placements as others, if that is important to you, though they might still be connected to their own former advisor's network.

Senior faculty

Senior faculty members have longer track records and there's a better chance they are a known name in the field. They will have more experience and are likely to have access to more funding, plus a stronger voice in the university's decision-making process. If you're looking for faculty assistance with job placement after graduation, senior professors are likely to have the largest network of former advisees and colleagues around the field.

The downside to a senior faculty member is that they typically no longer have the pressure to perform, so they may be less active - particularly if they are close to retirement. Sometimes, they may hold additional responsibilities or titles that take away time they have to spend with advisees. They can be set in their ways and not as willing to work with fresh ideas. They are also the least likely to be familiar with recent technology or proficient in English.

Mid-career

Mid-career faculty members combine the positives and negatives of the earlier categories. They will typically be a little more established than a junior faculty member and have earned some recognition within the field. But they're not at the top and will probably still be seeking further advancement, so there will be pressure on them to remain active.

In terms of negatives, they combine lesser degrees of the other two groups. Mid-career faculty members might be at a higher risk of taking a sabbatical than either of the other groups, but there's really no way that you can tell that in advance.

Advisees

You won't be able to find information about students that professor has advised in the past on Researchmap, but you may find it on their lab website, personal website, or university website.

If you can find information about current or past advisees, try to find out what their thesis or dissertation topics were and compare them to your own topic. If the professor has supervised similar thesis topics to what you want to research, that is a good sign that they will be a fit for your studies, as well.

STEP 3: RESEARCH THE UNIVERSITIES

By this time you should have a good understanding of all the potential supervisors on your list. You might even be tempted to prioritize them already, but there is one more important step to go through first.

It's time to look at the other half of the "university-professor" pair: The university. This is the moment of truth, so to speak: Is your professor affiliated with a graduate program taught in English.

From your previous research, you should know the name of the university and graduate school that each of your potential supervisors is affiliated with, so it's time to examine those programs. A Google search for the university and graduate school name should take you to the page with ease.

Since you are already familiar with your potential supervisor's research field, you do not need to spend too much time examining the program contents. But you need to make sure that the program is taught in English!

The best way to find out the program language is to look for the admissions requirements for fee-paying applicants. Those requirements will tell you if it is possible to enroll without Japanese language ability and what programs or tracks within the graduate school accept students for English-language programs. If you can't find any admissions requirements or application information in English, that usually shows that Japanese language ability is required.

If only particular tracks or majors within the graduate school are taught in English, make sure that your potential advisor is affiliated with one of those majors. You can check this by looking for the faculty profiles on the university website or an online syllabus, if there is one available in English. Your advisor must be from the same department/major where you enroll.

What to do if your potential supervisor is not affiliated with an English-language program

Do not give up just yet! If you remember earlier, I mentioned there is a way to work with faculty members who are in Japanese programs.

To do this, you need to find the closest possible English-taught program at that university. For example, I worked at a university that had a Graduate School of Pharmaceutical Sciences and a Graduate School of Sport and Health Sciences that only taught programs in Japanese, but also had a Graduate School of Life Sciences that taught programs in English. When applicants who only spoke English approached us about wanting to study under a professor in one of the Japanese-taught programs, we would recommend them to find an advisor in the Graduate School of Life Sciences, enroll in that graduate school, then work collaboratively with that professor as well as the faculty member in the Japanese-taught program they were interested in.

Of course, this work-around is going to require a little more complicated communication when you reach out to potential supervisors directly, so I would only recommend it if you are really passionate about working with that supervisor, but it is possible.

Recording your results

Once you have looked up your potential advisor's program language, add that to your table.

STEP 4: PRIORITIZE

At this point, you should have your university-professor list, have narrowed it down to the professors affiliated with English-taught programs (or programs where you can find a work-around as described in the previous section), and also have a pretty clear idea of each potential advisor's suitability to oversee your research.

Now it is time to prioritize them. If you are using a spreadsheet to keep track of your advisor research, you can add a "ranking" column to organize it. Otherwise, transfer your results into a clean list, in priority order, for easy reference later.

If you are planning to apply for the Embassy-Recommended MEXT Scholarship, you will need a list of three universities and professors for your application. If you're applying for the University-Recommended MEXT Scholarship, you can only apply to one university and one supervisor there. However, in either case, you'll want to have more targets than that for now.

In the second half of this book, I will walk you through getting into contact with your potential advisors in Japan. During that step, you may find that professors are unresponsive or that they are unwilling or unable to supervise your research. If that happens, you will need to have alternatives in mind.

So, when you make your list, do not stop at one or three names. Keep going and prioritize all the potential advisors you have identified so far.

Keep in mind, too, that you can only ever be in touch with one professor at any university at one time. If you have multiple professors that you are interested in working with at one university, even if they are in different graduate schools, choose the one best fit. If you have done your research, you should always be able to prioritize them. You will only be able to reach out to the others if that first choice professor does not work out.

PROGRESS CHECK

You should now have a list of target university-professor pairs for your MEXT Scholarship application, ranked in priority order. Congratulations! It's been a lot of work to get to this point.

You are halfway done with this book. But before you move on to actually contacting professors, it's time to shift gears and go back to your academic research.

Your next step is to write your Field of Study and Research Program Plan, targeting it at your first choice professor. When we started this book, you should have had your research question. Now, look at it again and make sure it is similar enough to your potential advisor's research. If not, think about what you can do to make it closer, so that your advisor will not only be able to supervise your research but also be excited to have you as their advisee.

With that knowledge and focus in mind, finish writing your Field of Study and Research Program Plan.

If you need to know more about how to write your Field of Study and Research Program Plan, I have a few articles about the format on my website, and the second book in this *Mastering the MEXT Scholarship Series* will walk you through the process of writing it, from idea to finished proposal. You can find more information at the links below:

Book: How to Write a Scholarship-Winning Field of Study and Research Program Plan

https://www.transenzjapan.com/blog/mastering-the-mext-scholarship/how-to-write-a-scholarship-winning-field-of-study-and-research-program-plan/

Article: "Field of Study and Research Program Plan: 2019-2020 MEXT Scholarship - Updated"

*This article covers the new format for the Field of Study and Research Program Plan introduced in 2019 for the Embassy-Recommended MEXT Scholarship.
https://www.transenzjapan.com/blog/field-of-study-and-research-program-plan-2019-2020-mext-scholarship-updated/

Article: "MEXT Scholarship Field of Study and Research Program Plan Elements"

*This article covers the "old" format of the Field of Study and Research Program Plan, which is still being used for the University-Recommended MEXT Scholarship, as of the 2020-2021 application cycle.
https://www.transenzjapan.com/blog/mext-scholarship-field-of-study-and-research-program-plan-elements/

What to do next

Once you have finished your Field of Study and Research Program Plan and gotten it to where you would be comfortable showing it to a potential future advisor in Japan, read on to the next chapter: How to Make Initial Contact.

EXERCISES

Most of the work that you will do in this chapter works best in a spreadsheet, and I have included a template in the bonus downloadable worksheets.

https://www.transenzjapan.com/mext/uniprofexercises

Basics

1. Brainstorm a list of all the potential keywords related to your research that you can use to search for potential advisors in Japan.

Potential advisor list

I recommend using the spreadsheet you can download from the link above for this process, but if you don't want to use that sheet, you can make your own list, starting with the columns below.

- Name
- Research focus area
- Name of affiliated university & graduate school
- Link to personal profile or website
- Contact information

2. From your previous literature review, identify all the authors in the works you reviewed who are affiliated with Japanese universities and add them to your list. (Just the names, for now.)

3. Go through the citations from the works in your literature review and add any authors of relevant cited works who teach at universities in Japan.

(Again, just the names.)

4. Search Researchmap using the keywords in question 1, above, and check the profiles of each researcher from the search results. Add any that have similar research fields to your own to your list.

5. Review journals and e-journals in your field from the past year and read the abstracts of any articles related to your research that you find. Research the authors of those articles and add them to your list if they are affiliated with a Japanese university.

6. Google your keywords from question 1, along with the words "university Japan". If you find any new faculty members at Japanese universities researching in your field, add them to your list.

7. Consult with your personal network for any additional names of researchers in your field who are active in Japan. Research those faculty members and add them to your list. Mark a star next to these researchers' names to show that you have a network connection to them for potential introduction later.

Advanced faculty research

8. Add the columns below to your table of potential advisors and use Researchmap, Google Scholar, or their personal websites to fill in the information, if possible:

- Number of publications or presentations in last three years
- Percentage of publications or presentations in English
- Number of citations in last five years (Google Scholar)
- Years since bachelor's degree
- Rank (Professor/Associate Professor, etc.)

- Similar thesis topics among advisees (yes / no)

University program research

9. Add a "Program Language" column to your table and record whether the program is offered in English or Japanese.

10. If the program is taught in Japanese but there is a related program offered in English where you could enroll and still work with that supervisor, add a column for "Related English Program" and write the name of the program taught in English. Research a potential advisor in that program and add that professor to your list as a separate entry, filling in all the relevant details from the questions above.

Prioritize

11. If using a spreadsheet, add a "Rank" column to your list (I recommend adding it on the left) and prioritize your potential supervisors in the order that you think you would like to work with them. If you are not using a spreadsheet, I recommend creating a new list, where you include only the information below. Write your professors in that list in your priority order.

- University Name
- Graduate School Name
- Professor Name
- Program Website
- MEXT Scholarship Application Information Page
- Professor's Contact Information

CHAPTER FOUR: HOW TO MAKE INITIAL CONTACT

W elcome back!

If you are preparing in advance and followed my instructions at the end of the last chapters, then between reading those chapters and this one, you should have finished writing your Field of Study and Research Program Plan.

If you are reading this during the application process or already had your Field of Study and Research Program Plan complete, maybe you're reading straight through.

Where you should be

In either case, you should have a complete Field of Study and Research Program Plan - something that you would be comfortable showing to a potential advisor in Japan - as well as your prioritized list of professors that you would like to work with.

As you progress through this next chapter, you will make initial contact with your target professors. Before we get there, though, we'll cover:

- Essential preparation
- How to find contact information for professors in Japan
- Creating your communication strategy (for contacting before or during the application process)
- Sample first email templates

By the end of those steps, you will be ready to hit send or, sometimes, start dialing.

Let's get started!

BEFORE YOU START REACHING OUT

Before you contact universities or professors in Japan, we are going to take some time to go through essential preparation steps, like preparing your email account and yourself for professional communication. I'll also cover some pitfalls that can ruin your relationship and chances with a supervisor in Japan before you start.

Setting up Your Email Account

First, let's talk about technical details. These are some of the easiest to get out of the way.

Professional email address

If you are enrolled at a university, I recommend you use your university email account when you reach out to universities and potential advisors in Japan. Your university email account should already look professional, with your full name as the sender name and a professional signature block. (Though just to be sure, you can read on below for my recommendations on account settings.)

A university email account is also likely to be "trusted" by receiving email servers and result in fewer problems such as your email being filtered as spam, even if you have links or attachments included. The exception to this is if your university's email server has been hacked recently and used to send out spam emails. Avoid using your university email account if you have seen a message from your university IT department during the past two to three weeks warning that the university email has been hacked.

If you are using a personal account, such as a Gmail account or other free web service, or your own server for a personal website, then take a few minutes to make sure that your email address, sender information, and signature block are professional.

For your email address, an address with your first and last name is best. First initial and last name, or something similar, works equally well. But if your email address is something "cute" or overly casual, such as including the name of your favorite *anime* character, or an irreverent nickname, then I highly recommend getting a new email address for this application. I have seen applicants with a wide range of email addresses, from Studio Ghibli characters to rude references to parts of the anatomy. Around the office, those applicants became known by their email addresses and it was hard to take them seriously. Make your new address your first and last name, and you will have no problems with professionalism. If you use a service like Gmail, then you can set up your new email address to auto-forward to your old email account. That way, you do not need to constantly check the new account. You'll know when messages arrive, then you can log in to that new account and write a reply.

Your sender name

Regardless of your eventual choice for your email address, your "sender name", the name that shows up next to your email subject line in the recipient's inbox, should be your first and last name. Including a middle name or initial is also fine, if that is what you go by. I recommend capitalizing the first letter of each name.

Your signature block

Most email services allow you to include a signature block that goes out with every email by default. You do not need to use this, and in most cases it isn't necessary for the MEXT scholarship application, as long as you take the time to type your name at the end of each message, which you absolutely should do, even if you have a signature block.

The more important factor is what *not* to put in your signature block!

I recommend you do not include multiple links, even if they are to your various social media accounts. An email that includes multiple links is more likely to look like spam and get automatically filtered before it even reaches your target supervisor. (Trust me, I used to include links to all of my social media accounts in all of my TranSenz emails and many of them ended up getting filtered as spam - even messages to myself!)

I also recommend that you avoid bright colors or unusual fonts. If you include a quote in your signature block, then I recommend something academic and related to your field of study. Just like with the email address itself, try to avoid being too cute or casual. Think about the first impression your quote will make on a professor who doesn't yet know you.

The last thing I recommend you avoid is anything like "Sent from my smartphone." Some smartphone email apps will add this automatically, but if yours does, disable it, or better yet, don't email from your smartphone. There is no situation under which "Sent from my smartphone" can make a positive impression, and there's a decent chance that it could make a negative one, as there are some professors who will see it as a sign that you did not consider the message important enough to sit down at a computer to write a reply. Smartphone "autocorrect" features are also notorious for resulting in inappropriate messages, so be careful!

I'll close with one thing that can be beneficial to have in your email signature: Pronouns. Recently, it has become a trend to include your preferred pronouns in your signature block (e.g. He/Him/His). While I understand this is often an expression of gender identity, it is also really helpful if you are emailing someone from a different culture who might not guess your gender based on your name!

Spam and inbox filters

If you use an inbox filtering service like "Boxbe", don't. Stop it right away if you ever hope to get a response from your prospective supervisor in Japan. If you don't know what Boxbe is, it's a service that sends a reply email to anyone who tries to write to you asking them to add themselves to your acceptable senders list. It's probably supposed to protect against spam, but it also "protects" against legitimate people emailing you. If a professor has to go through additional trouble to get an email through to you, assume that they're just going to give up.

What about spam filters? Before you try to contact a potential advisor in Japan, or anyone at a university, I recommend you add the advisor's specific email address and the university's email domain (everything after the "@" mark in the email address) as a whole to your "trusted senders" list, "whitelist", "never send to spam list" or whatever your particular email service calls it.

If you do not know how to do this, do a quick Google search for "how to whitelist an email address" and the name of your email provider. You should be able to find simple step-by-step instructions.

Reply settings

On most email services, you have a choice whether to include all previous emails in your reply. I recommend you turn it on. (If you are using Thunderbird, make sure you have it set so that previous emails appear *under* your reply.) When you are emailing back and forth with professors, they might not always remember who you are, especially in early messages. Including the text of previous replies can help them easily refer to your communication history as necessary.

Alerts and reply timing

You never want to miss a reply from your potential supervisor, or let it go too long without a reply. I will talk about the appropriate time to take between replies in a later section, but even when you want to wait to reply, that should be deliberate, not because you haven't noticed.

If you can check your email on a smartphone or other device that you carry with you, then I recommend setting up push notifications, so that you always know when a message arrives. That way you can plan your reply accordingly. (Remember, you should avoid *sending* your email from a smartphone, but it is not a bad idea to check new messages with one.)

If you do not check your email on a smartphone, then at least be sure that you make a schedule to check once each day.

Professional Communication

The next step after getting your technical setup prepared is your mentality. All the steps that we went through in the previous section were about professional communications, so hopefully you've already realized that applies to the contents of your email, as well. In this section, we're going to make sure that you have mentally prepared yourself for professional communication with your future advisor in Japan so you will not get off on the wrong foot.

Over my decade working with the MEXT scholarship, I have seen some horrible communications from applicants. They range from poorly planned and confusing messages to emails that were downright rude. Even now, most of the emails I get from readers of my blog are bad enough to make me wince. Here's one common example.

"Please sir, I need this scholarship. How can I get?"

That's it. The entire message. I can already tell that this person doesn't have a chance - at least, not without a significant mindset shift and months of work. Of course, I'm not a professor and not someone you need to be formal with, but email etiquette should apply to every message you send, particularly related to the MEXT scholarship, if for no other reason than to get yourself in practice.

But I know you're better than that. After all, you're already this far into reading at least one book about preparing for the scholarship and following along with the exercises. That tells me you have a professional mindset and so most of what I discuss below is going to be natural to you. But just in case, let's review what a potential advisor in Japan - or an administrative office - is going to expect from your communication.

Basic mindset

Write each email as if it is to someone who has the power to give you one million dollars and a life-changing experience - because they do! That's how much the MEXT Scholarship can be worth to an applicant who starts as a research student and proceeds through the Master's and Doctorate, between stipends and tuition benefits.

Put yourself in the recipient's shoes for a minute. You are not just asking this person to help you get a life-changing scholarship; you are also asking this person to take personal responsibility for you - someone they don't know and from a country/culture they may not be familiar with - for at least two years. That's an enormous commitment and every communication from you will factor into their decision whether or not you are someone they can work with. If you are polite, clear, self-sufficient, and easy for them to work with, that will help them say yes!

When I handled MEXT scholarship applications at my university, I can remember several examples of applicants that I hoped would fail because they were so demanding or rude in their emails. I did not want to have to continue dealing with those applicants for two to five years once they started studying!

Now, I'm not saying that you have to be obsequious or subservient, just respectful.

Subject line

Your subject line should let the person know what your goal is before they open your email. Usually, this is something that you only need to think about in the first email, since subsequent replies will keep the same subject line throughout.

Email format

Think of your emails as a professional letter that happens to be written electronically, not as a glorified, long-form text message. Especially among the typical faculty age group, email came about as a replacement for mail, so the courtesies of written letters still apply. A message that sounds like an SMS, especially if it contains shorthand like "2" for "to" or other such nonsense, is going to leave a childish, immature, and unprepared impression.

That means that each letter should start with a salutation, such as "Dear Prof. Sato,". Never start a letter with, "Hi" or without a salutation at all, even in subsequent messages.

If is fine to address your potential advisor as "professor", even if you know they are an Associate Professor or Assistant Professor. I have never known anyone to get insulted by that. Another option is to address them as "Dear Sato-Sensei", but I would recommend saving that for a second or third email, once you know them better.

Following your salutation, you should split your email into several brief paragraphs for clarity and ease of reading. Don't lump everything together in one block of text.

Your first paragraph will be one to two sentences to restate the purpose of your email. Then you'll have one or two paragraphs to explain. Your last paragraph should include a call to action (what you want the recipient to do after reading your email, such as reply).

Include a closing salutation, such as "Sincerely" or "Regards", then your name. Finally, include your email address below your name, as well.

Yes, this probably sounds obvious, but you would be surprised how few applicants actually write well-formatted, polite emails.

Customized emails for each recipient

You should write each email to each potential university separately and customize the content to your recipient. This is especially true in your initial contact.

In the earlier chapters of this book, we researched each individual professor and their current research interests. When you contact them, be sure to briefly reflect that research in your message. Mention the professor and university (as well as the specific graduate school, if appropriate) by name in the message, and refer to why you want to work with that specific professor.

Never, ever, send the same message to multiple universities, especially not at the same time! Your messages should never be so general that it would even be possible to send them to more than one person.

Offer value

Too often, MEXT scholarship applicants focus only on what is in it for them. You want a scholarship; you want to spend your next few years living in Japan - or maybe your entire career; you want to leverage your education to make a difference. Of course, that's normal. But you also need to think about what's in it for the other person. A relationship needs to have value for all parties.

In my book *How to Apply for the MEXT Scholarship*, I talked about why MEXT offers this scholarship and how it benefits Japan, so that you could use that understanding to appeal to the scholarship reviewers in your application by showing how you will contribute to their goals (while, of course, earning the degree that means so much to you!)

When you approach potential advisors, you need to consider the same: What is in it for them? What benefit can you bring them as an advisee? You will express your value in how you can contribute to their research. If you are applying in a STEM field, then you will probably work on a research project that supports the lab's overall goals, so this will be relatively easy to describe. Even in social sciences, focusing on the areas of overlap between your research and your potential advisor's, as well as your intent to publish your findings, also implies benefits to the professor, their research, and their standing in the field.

Keep it simple . . .

KISS is an acronym for basic communication philosophy. I'll let you guess what that final "s" stands for. It isn't necessarily a polite word.

That means your email should be short, clear, and to the point. You don't want the recipient to be confused about what you want, or to struggle to understand any of your sentences. That will leave a negative impression. In a later section, we will go through your email communication strategy, including how to build each message around a specific goal or action that you want the recipient to take. For now, remember that your emails should be short and focused. A short, simple message is much easier to reply to and has a better chance of establishing a pattern of communication.

Proofreading

Don't just rely on the automatic spell-checker in your email software, if you have one. Proofread every email before you send it. An email with spelling or grammar errors comes across as unprofessional, unprepared, and uncaring about your recipient. It can also lead to serious confusion and the wrong direction for your research relationship.

There's a joke that goes, "I do my best proofreading after I hit 'send'." Don't let that be you! Check your message carefully, first. If you are not confident about your writing, ask someone else to look at it, too.

If you use Gmail, there's a setting you can activate that actually keeps the email from sending for a prescribed amount of time after you hit send - I have mine set to 10 seconds - so that you have time for a last-last second check, and the ability to cancel it. But never rely only on that.

Language

If you are planning to study in English, write your messages to your potential supervisor in English. If you write in Japanese, you might accidentally create the false expectation that you will study in Japanese, which could lead to problems later. It is fine to mix in a Japanese greeting, if you're confident and familiar with Japanese email etiquette, but avoid anything casual, like こんにちは, or using language that you learned from your favorite *anime* or *manga*.

If you do plan to study in Japanese and want to communicate in that language, be sure that you set up your computer to type in Japanese. Never send a letter written entirely in *rômaji*. That's just painful to read.

Links and attachments

An email with multiple links and attachments risks being filtered as spam, so keep them down to a minimum. I recommend a maximum of one link, such as to a website detailing your research experience, or one attachment, such as a one-page CV. This is especially important in early emails, before you have a history of contacting one another, but any email can be caught by a spam filter.

Remember, too, that links and attachments are subtle demands of the recipient's time. It is better than including everything in the body of your email, since opening a link or attachment is ultimately optional, but it still implies you want the person to read them. If you include links or attachments, make sure you have a specific purpose for doing so.

Finally, if you mention an attachment in your email, be sure that you have actually attached the file! It is embarrassing for everyone involved if your potential advisor needs to write back to ask you to send the missing attachment.

Expectations

Even though I have described several principles that you should keep in mind for your communication, do not expect the professor to adhere to the same. You are the one asking the professor for help and are probably in touch with only three potential advisors at once. They are dealing with their own current advisees as well as potentially multiple applicants on top of their teaching and research. So, you might get just a brief, informal reply.

If that happens, do not treat it as an invitation to drop the formality in your emails, at least not until you have met the potential advisor in person and established a relationship.

So, now that we've covered some basic principles, let's look at a few examples of what not to do - things that can ruin your chances at establishing a relationship before you even get started.

How to Fail

Before we move on, I want to cover a few examples I have seen that can ruin your chances of establishing a relationship before it even starts. Some of these might seem painfully obvious, or might seem obvious once you think about them, but I have seen examples of each of these in actual applications. So, there was someone out there who thought it was a good idea.

The generic email

I used to see this all the time when I was the first point of contact for all scholarship inquiries at my university.

"Dear Professor,
    I would be most honored to study at your esteemed university. . ."

Okay, it sounds polite, right? No. Not at all. The applicant couldn't even be bothered to fill in the name of the professor and university. Plus, in my case, they were emailing an admin office address, not a specific professor, so they did not write the message with the recipient in mind. This kind of message broadcasts that you are sending the same message to multiple universities and haven't done any kind of research on your own.

But that brings me to an example that is even worse:

Multiple addresses in the "To" field

I have received emails like the one above that were sent simultaneously to 10 different universities. I could tell because all the addresses were there in the "To" field.

As I mentioned earlier, you should never write an email so generic that you could send it to multiple professors, so this shouldn't be an issue. But if a professor can see that you're writing to multiple people at once, they know you are not committed to working with them, or even doing any basic research, so it is not worth their time to reply. Even when they know you are likely in contact with other universities, each professor wants to know that you are committed enough to write them a personal message.

Demanding emails

Believe it or not, I have received emails with the subject line "Demand for scholarship offer". I think most of these emails have come from native French speakers, since "demande" in French translates to "request" in English, but to my French-speaking readers out there, this is an example of a *faux amis* - a false friend. Do not translate "demande" to "demand"!

But beyond simple translation errors, I have often seen emails that are demanding or presumptuous. One example is applicants writing that they "need" a Letter of Acceptance. Even saying something like "I would appreciate it very much if you could write me a Letter of Acceptance for my MEXT scholarship application" is rude, because it assumes the professor will do so, when they know nothing about you. Remember what I mentioned in the last section: Asking for a Letter of Acceptance is the same as asking this potential advisor to take personal responsibility for you for the next two to four years. That's a lot to ask in a first email.

Instead, start by expressing interest in studying under the professor and ask for their time and consideration of you as an advisee. Even when you are up against a deadline and need a response quickly, always ask to the professor to consider your application *then* give you a Letter of Acceptance if they are willing to supervise you.

Begging

This relates to the previous mistake, but asking nicely isn't enough to get the professor to agree to supervise you. Yes, you want to be polite, and "please" is never out of place, but the mistake comes in starting and ending your argument with a polite request.

You need to make an appeal based on the academic merit of your research and also mention the potential benefit to the advisor of working with you.

Being unclear

If your message does not state a simple message and invite a specific response, you are making it difficult for the other person to get back to you.

I have been on the receiving end of emails that were essentially a long essay about the sender's past research. They ramble all over the place about the different things they have studied, leaving me thinking in half a dozen directions at once. Sometimes, I couldn't tell what the applicant wanted to study in Japan - I wasn't even sure the applicant knew - and worse, many of these emails ended without a clear call to action.

When you write an email, make sure it is focused on what you want to research in Japan and particularly how that research interest relates to the professor that you are contacting. When you reach the end of the email, put in a clear call to action, something that tells the recipient what you want them to do next. Often, in a first email, that will be to reply to show if they are interested in your research topic so that you can send them more information or set up a direct conversation on Zoom, Skype, etc.

If you're not sure if your message is sufficiently clear, test it on someone. Get an honest friend to read it and tell you what they think it's saying and what they would do next.

Lazy questions

I cannot tell you how often I get questions to which an applicant could have found the answer themselves within five minutes. It's called the MEXT Scholarship for *Research* Students, but applicants consistently fail to do even the most basic research about the application process on the university or embassy website - or even on my website.

Now, I write advice articles about how to apply for the MEXT scholarship, so I don't mind these questions. But I shudder every time I get them, because I think, "What if this person treats their potential advisor the same way?" If you ask your future advisor a question that you could have looked up on the university website, that will not leave a positive impression. It tells them you are lazy, not self-sufficient, and are going to be a lot of work to supervise.

You should also make sure you are asking your questions to the right person. Do not ask a professor questions about administrative details, like housing, or scholarship payment schedules. That's not something the professor would know, and it is going to take them just as much work to find the answer as it would take you. Figure out the correct administrative office to contact and ask directly.

But administrative details are not the worst thing you can ask a professor.

Asking the professor to propose a research topic

If you've come this far in the book, I assume this isn't a problem for you. But, yes, I have seen it. I have had applicants ask me how to get in touch with a professor so that they can propose a research topic for them. Wrong order.

If you do not have something that you want to research, then you probably need to think hard about why you want to go to graduate school in the first place. You should always have your research problem in mind before contacting a prospective advisor, even if you might change that research topic in consultation with your advisor later. Let the professor know you are willing to accept their advice and guidance on changing your topic as necessary, but if you don't show the initiative to come up with a topic in the first place, you are broadcasting that you are not proactive and will be a lot of work to supervise.

Spelling and grammar errors

If you can't compose a competent email, what is the professor on the receiving end going to think about your ability to write a thesis?

Always check for spelling and grammar, including the subject line and any names. Have another human proofread your messages. Like I said in the previous section, do not rely on your email software to do it for you.

I do not think you would do any of these things deliberately. But take a moment now to think about whether you might do any of them unconsciously, and take steps to fix them.

HOW TO GET IN CONTACT WITH YOUR TARGET PROFESSOR

Before we work on your communication strategy, let's make sure of one thing: Can you get in touch with your target advisor?

Hopefully, by now, you've found their contact information during your background research. If you have, great, you can skip this section.

The same goes for if you have a connection who can introduce you. If that's the case, and someone is willing to write an email on your behalf, move on to planning what you want that email to say and what you will say in your follow-up messages.

But what if you haven't found an email address yet?

How to search for contact information

My first recommendation is to find it on your own. If you can't find an email address, at least try for a phone number.

Search the university website for your target advisor and see if you can find their email address or phone extension listed. Try searching for their name on the university website in both English and Japanese. A faculty or researcher database can be a great resource if the university has one online.

If the university has an online syllabus, search there for courses that your professor teaches. You might find their contact information in a course syllabus. If not, see if you can at least find other professors' email addresses and try to find any patterns. For example, does every professor have an email that is their first initial followed by the first seven letters of their last name? If there's a pattern there, you might use it to guess your professor's email.

Check the professor's lab or personal website, too, if they have one. You might find their contact information, or at least a contact form, there.

If that doesn't work, it's time to go broader on Google. Try searching for the professor's name and the university's domain (e.g. "u-tokyo.ac.jp"). You might find their contact information from a forgotten CV on a conference website. If the professor has their own website, try searching for their name and that site's domain, too, in case they have an email address there. You can also try searching for the professor's name and university name. Don't forget to try their name in Japanese, too!

First contact by phone

Sometimes your search will not yield an email address, but might net you a phone number. In that case, consider making your first contact attempt by phone. With VOIP phone services like Skype Out, you can call phone numbers in other countries with a minimal charge. If you reach out by phone and your potential advisor answers, then that also has the benefit of being a lot harder to ignore than an email.

If you reach out by phone, be prepared to discuss your research interest, in case your professor has the time and invites it. But that should not be your primary goal right away. Your first goal should be to establish whether the professor is interested in talking further. After a brief introduction, like you would do in the first email that we'll discuss later, ask if you can follow up to send more information by email and ask for their address.

It's important that you ask for their contact information and be the one to reach out to them! Do not leave the next step in their hands if you can avoid it. Once you have that contact information, be sure to send your message as quickly as possible.

Contacting through the university

If you have exhausted every means to find the professor's direct contact information with no result, then you can also reach out to them through the administrative office of their graduate school.

It should be much easier to find the email address for the administrative office of the graduate school where the professor works. That information is almost always going to be available on the university website. Once you have the contact information for the graduate school, you can write them with a polite request to either share the professor's email address with you (unlikely, if you could not find it posted anywhere so far) or to pass along a message to the professor. I recommend that you also include the message intended for the professor in the email!

So, what is that message going to say? We're about to work on that.

YOUR COMMUNICATION STRATEGY: NETWORKING IN ADVANCE

I am going to split the rest of the chapter into two halves. First, I will cover what to do if you are reaching out in advance to connect with your potential advisor before the application period. Then, I'll go through the same sections with advice on what to do if you are contacting them after the application has already started. In both cases, I will cover the following topics:

- Your communication strategy
- Writing your first email
- Templates for your first email

If the application process has already started for you, skip ahead to the section titled, "Your Communication Strategy: During the Application Process". Otherwise, read on!

Your goal

Like any other strategy, you must begin with your goal. What outcome do you hope to get from communicating with your target advisor?

Ultimately, your goal will be to earn the professor's support and agreement to supervise you. If your relationship develops far enough, you may even be able to ask the professor to review and offer feedback on your Field of Study and Research Program Plan. However, you do not need to get there in your first message! The reason you are reaching out in advance is to build a relationship gradually.

Your first goal should be simply to get a favorable reply and an expression of interest in learning more. That's it, but that is a significant milestone by itself. You should assume that at least a few of your outreach efforts will not get beyond this point. You might end up getting some hard "No"s. I'll talk more about how to deal with that in the next chapter, but once you get past that first positive reply, it gets easier.

With each subsequent email beyond the first, you're going to have a different goal. It might be to schedule a Zoom call to discuss your research with your professor, or to see if they will review your Field of Study and Research Program Plan. Or it could be simply to strengthen your relationship by showing your research progress. How you progress depends on the replies from your potential advisor.

Plan for each email

Each time you set fingers to keyboard, you should have a goal in mind for what you want to get out of the message. You should also have a plan for how to make your potential advisor want to give it to you! I hope that doesn't sound slimy or manipulative. It's quite the opposite. Because the best way to get someone to give you what you want is to find where your desire intersects with theirs and make the dialog about meeting their goals and needs at the same time as yours.

Fortunately for you, most professors have a strong desire to advance their research and standing in their field, and that's something that you can contribute to by completing the very research that drove you to apply for graduate school. If your research topic and your potential advisor's are similar enough, then the relationships and mutual support should develop naturally.

Message timing

One factor you want to consider in your emails in order to improve the possibility of a reply is timing - both in terms of time of year and time of day.

Often, you won't be able to control the time of year that you reach out. That is going to depend on when you're ready. But keep the Japanese academic calendar in mind and what it might mean for your likelihood of getting a prompt response.

The Japanese academic calendar runs from April to March. The semesters typically run from April to July and October to February. There are typically breaks in August/September and Late February/March. Of course, you should check the academic calendar for the specific universities that you want to apply to for precise details.

What does that mean for your contact? Well, if you reach out just before the beginning or just after the semester, you're likely to find the professor busy, with less time to communicate with applicants. They'll be working on finalizing class materials or grading. If you contact them during breaks, there is a chance they will be away from campus conducting research and may be less likely to be checking their email as often. Reaching out during the semesters can yield a better result. They will be more likely to be checking email daily and may have more time to reply to emails, such as during office hours if none of their students stop in.

I also recommend considering the time of day. Of course, this is important if you plan to reach out by phone, but it can also be a factor for email. If your email arrives during the professor's workday, they might see it right away and respond sooner. Gmail, at least, allows you to write an email in advance and set it to send at a later time. Setting your email to send during the morning on a Japanese weekday may help you get a response faster.

One last recommendation on planning your communication strategy

The ideas I have shared above come from working with applicants over the past decade, as well as scouring forums for successful examples and analyzing what they had in common. But this isn't the *only* way to do things. If you know anyone who has successfully earned the MEXT Scholarship in the past, I recommend that you reach out to them for advice on how they contacted their future advisor, as well! Every successful example (and even every unsuccessful one) helps.

But now, it's time to get down to the business of writing that first email.

THE FIRST EMAIL: NETWORKING IN ADVANCE

A lot of your success in reaching out to a potential supervisor depends on your first email. But while that sounds like a lot of pressure, don't panic. It's important, but it isn't complicated. I will provide a template below that you can use.

Remember, the goal of your initial email is just to get a favorable response. Even a neutral one will do. Think of it like going on a first date: You just want to find out if the person on the other end is interested in talking further. You are not trying to get married on day one, so to speak. If your future supervisor writes back with encouragement or even permission to send more information, that's a success!

So, how to we get there? Write a short, professional email with a clear message and call to action that is easy to reply to. Your initial email should cover the points below:

Introduce yourself

In one to two sentences, give your name, where you are from (university and country), and your research interest.

Explain your interest in them and offer value

This is the part that needs to be customized to each professor.

In a second paragraph of two to three sentences, explain why you are reaching out to that professor. Be specific! Citing one of their articles or presentations that you found interesting, or quoting a statement about their research interest from their university, lab, or personal website would be great here.

Try to make it something that is related to your research topic and explain why it interested you.

In your closing sentence of this paragraph, also try to state how you hope your research will contribute to your target supervisor's work.

Offer additional information and ask for a reply

In the third and final paragraph, close by asking if the professor can consider supervising you and offer additional details about your research interest to aid their decision. Offer to provide additional information in a follow-up email or a Zoom/Skype call, if the professor is willing.

That's it. That is all your first email needs to do. In fact, I would recommend not trying to do much more. But if you cannot resist, you can consider a single attachment or link. Remember, more attachments and links mean more of a risk of being sent to spam.

One attachment

I do not recommend attaching your Field of Study and Research Program Plan at this point. It's still too early. Wait until the professor gives a positive reply.

The best thing to attach at this point would be a simple one-page CV focused on your research and/or related professional background. I would not recommend going over a single page, since you still want this to be something that your potential supervisor can scan to aid their decision in whether to reply to you to ask for more information. There should be no need to go longer than one page unless you already have an extensive career or research and publication experience.

Your CV in this case does not need to cover every detail of your life, either. You should target it at that professor as a tool to achieve your goal. So it should only mention relevant details to your research topic and academic qualifications.

If you have your own website that is related to your research interest, you can include that link within the CV, as well.

Of course, as with your email itself, you want to make sure the CV is professional, well-formatted, and easy to read.

One link

Instead of including an attachment, the other approach would be to include a single link. This would work best if you have your own website showcasing your work related to your research topic, so it is an appropriate approach for applicants in fields such as fine arts and architecture who would have examples to showcase.

If you do not have a website or any examples of your past works or research to show off, then this is not a requirement, by any means. It is only something you should consider if you have a specific purpose to do so!

One example of this approach comes from Lars Martinson, one of the first successful MEXT Scholars to write about his application experience. Mr. Martinson applied in the field of Japanese line art, so he wanted to showcase his works to prospective supervisors for their consideration in that initial contact. He set up a simple web page with his background, research proposal, works, and download links. You can read about his process on his blog: http://larsmartinson.com/how-i-got-the-monbusho-research-scholarship-part-3-of-4/

His application was back in 2007, and there are many more tools available to us now for easy web design and customization. If you wanted to do something similar these days, you could create a separate page for each professor you planned to contact and embed a self-introduction video into the pages, as well.

Again, I only recommend this approach if a website showcasing your past works makes sense for your application and if you have the skills and resources to create such a page. Putting up a page just for the sake of having one will not help and could create a negative impression if it is irrelevant or poorly designed.

Sample Message: Networking in Advance

In the past section, I described what you should include in your initial email - and I also promised you a template which you can find below. I have also included this template in the downloadable bonus documents, so that you can copy/paste it from there into your own email.

* * *

Subject Line:

Master's Degree Applicant - Request for Supervision

Body:

Dear Professor Sato,

Please pardon me for reaching out to you suddenly.

My name is Travis Senzaki and I am a bachelor's degree student in community development studies at the University of Johannesburg, South Africa. My goal is to continue my education with a Master's degree in Environmental Policy & Rural Development studies at the Kyoto University Graduate School of Economics and I have a strong desire to work under your supervision, as my research is focused on the rehabilitation and development of former mining communities in Japan and South Africa.

I have followed your work in the field, particularly your research on the development of the Joban Hawaiian Center in the former mining community of Iwaki, and comparisons to how other communities in Japan transitioned to a post-mining economy, from "Post-Mining Transition: A Comparison of Community Approaches in Tohoku, Japan" in the *Journal of Rural Studies.* I would like to learn more about your ongoing research and contribute to it, as well, while I compare the situation there with examples from my home country of South Africa.

My goal is to start my master's degree in the Fall 2022 Semester, and I was hoping you would be willing and able to be my advisor, if I am able to obtain admission to your program. If you could consider that, I would be honored to have the opportunity to discuss my current and future research with you in more detail by email or by arranging a call on Zoom, Skype, etc., at your convenience.

Could you please let me know if that would be possible?

Thank you in advance for your kind consideration.
Regards,
Travis

Travis Senzaki
Pronouns: Him/Him/His
University of Johannesburg,

BA(Hons) Community Development, Class of 2021

travis@transenzjapan.com

* * *

Notes about the example

I have used my name as the sample candidate, and the degree programs are real (as is the example of Iwaki, Fukushima), but that wasn't my academic background. Professor Sato (the most common last name in Japan) is fictional, as is the research title and journal. The point is to give an example of the level of detail you should aim for in this message and the important items to cover.

The subject line in the example is something that you can copy and use as-is, though you might want to give it your own personal touch. If too many people contact the same professor with the same subject line, it might look odd to the recipient.

The initial greeting is a loose translation of the Japanese phrase that would be common when emailing a person who you do not know with no introduction. It may sound a little humble, but a Japanese professor should recognize it, and it will hint right away that you have some familiarity with Japanese culture.

In the first paragraph, I introduced myself and my academic background, as well as my goal and why I was reaching out to the professor, including my specific research problem and my desire to work under their supervision. This paragraph would need to be customized for each professor I contacted, to include the specific university and program name.

In the second paragraph, I described my interest in the professor, including his/her academic field and a specific publication. I also mentioned at the end that I hope to contribute to the professor's research. I did not go into specific detail, but the point in including that line was to show that I have an interest in contributing, not just being on the receiving end of advice.

In the third paragraph, I described what I wanted out of this email - confirmation that the professor could supervise me and the opportunity to discuss further - I also offered more information. Finally, I included a specific question alone on a final line, making it as easy as possible for the professor to write a reply.

My closing greeting was thanks for the professor's time, not a request or push for a reply or any other attempt to pressure the professor. I want to leave them knowing that I appreciate the time they have given already in reading my message. Besides, I already have the question above and repeating something like "I look forward to your favorable reply" here could come across as demanding and pressuring.

I did not include links or attachments in this email, as in the case of this sample applicant, it would be unlikely that he would have any relevant works to share or significant academic background a CV could highlight. If I did, I would have described them either in the third paragraph or in a postscript below my signature block.

Your turn

If you haven't done so already, it's time for you to write your first emails to your target professors. You do not need to match my template above, but try to keep your messages short and to the point, as I have done in the example and make sure that you cover the relevant points.

There is a place in the worksheets for this, but, of course, you are free to type it directly into your email program, as well! Once you finish, have someone else review it for clarity.

The remaining sections of this chapter cover communication strategies, the initial email, and a sample message for applicants who are reaching out for the first time during the application process, so you can skip them and go directly to the next chapter, which is all about how to handle different replies and follow-up communication with your professors.

YOUR COMMUNICATION STRATEGY: DURING THE APPLICATION PROCESS

If you are reaching out to professors for the first time after the application process has started, you have less flexibility with both your schedule and your ability to change your research topic based on the professor's response. That's the negative. The positive side of that is that it makes your communication task much more straightforward: You need to find a professor who is willing and able to supervise the research topic you have already proposed in your Field of Study and Research Program Plan.

For the Embassy-Recommended MEXT Scholarship, there are two points during the application process where it makes sense to reach out to target professors: The first is before you submit your application to the embassy. Usually, this would be after you complete your Field of Study and Research Program Plan, but before your fill in your Placement Preference Form. At this point, you would be trying to evaluate professors to see which ones to list in your Placement Preference Form, as well as trying to establish a relationship that you can reference in your interview. The second time you might contact professors is after you have passed the Primary Screening, when you are applying for Letters of Provisional Acceptance. In either case, though, I assume it is too late for you to change your Field of Study and Research Program Plan contents.

For the University-Recommended MEXT Scholarship, when you reach out to professors in the application process depends on the instructions from the university that you are applying to. But as with the embassy example, above, it will probably be at the point where you can no longer change your research proposal.

Your communication strategy will need to account for this inflexibility.

Your goal

Every strategy begins with knowing your goal, as well as the goals of each step along the way.

When you are contacting professors during the application process, your goal is to gauge their ability and willingness to supervise your research as quickly as possible. Unlike the example of contacting professors in advance, you are not trying to build a relationship gradually - though you will want to strengthen your relationship after you get that initial approval - you are seeking a quick decision. If the professor cannot supervise you, it helps to know as soon as possible so that you can move on.

That means your emails should focus on determining whether there is a possibility of acceptance quickly. You will need to be up front about your situation, your timeline, and your interest.

Plan for each email

It is likely that you won't have much time to exchange emails back and forth, so it is important that you know what you want to get out of each email and plan the contents to make it easy for the potential advisor to give it to you.

Your first email should start with the goal of determining whether the professor is willing to consider taking you on as a student. Keep in mind that you just want them to be willing to "consider" it, not necessarily commit to advising you. You will also want to pave the way for a second communication, either by email or a direct conversation, where you will get their final decision.

Timing

If you're reaching out to potential supervisors after the application has already started, then the best time to contact them is right away! As soon as you have all of your materials and your email prepared, I recommend you send your message as early as possible.

However, I recommend you consider the time of day. If possible, send your email so that it arrives during the morning of a Japanese workday. If your professor gets your email during the workday, there is a better chance that it will get immediate attention, but if it arrives at night or on a weekend, then it might be one of several messages in the inbox when the professor next checks, and might not get prioritized. Gmail, at least, has a function that allows you to prepare an email in advance and set it to send at a specific time. But if your email does not have that option, you can always wait until the appropriate time to click "send", even if that means waking up in the middle of the night.

THE FIRST EMAIL: DURING THE APPLICATION PROCESS

Unlike reaching out to professors in advance to build a relationship, if you are contacting them during the application process, then there may be rules for your contact. I recommend that you review the university's website, first, before contacting professors, to see if there are any guidelines that you might need to follow. For example, they may ask that you attach all of your application documents, or that you contact the professors in a certain way. If they do, follow those instructions.

The best way to find out if universities have specific requirements or guidelines for contacting professors is to do a Google search for "Monbukagakusho Scholarship" and the university's name. You can also try "MEXT Scholarship". Those searches should help you find the page on the university's website with instructions for you.

The description and sample message below assume that the university is telling you only to reach out to potential supervisors to get their approval with no additional requirements.

When I wrote about building a relationship in advance in the previous section, I said that your first email should be like a first date - you're just trying to get to know the person, not get married on day one. But if you're making contact for the first time during the application process, then that analogy no longer applies.

Instead, think of your approach like an elevator pitch. In marketing, an elevator pitch is an explanation of your product or idea that is short enough and appealing enough that you could deliver it within the span of an elevator ride, if you found yourself in the same car as the person you are trying to sell to. It gives that person enough information to decide whether they are interested and want to know more, in a way that encourages the result you want.

Keep in mind, though, that it's not a bad thing to get a "no". Sometimes, a quick "no" can be a good thing. If a professor cannot supervise you, or if your research on that professor was misleading and they aren't a good choice to supervise your research, then you want to get that "no" quickly, so that you can move on to approach a professor who will be a better fit.

Here's what your first email should accomplish:

Introduce yourself

In one to two sentences, give your name, your academic background, and your research interest. In this case, you want to let them know up front you are applying for the MEXT scholarship.

Explain your interest in them and offer value

This is the part that needs to be customized to each professor.

In a second paragraph of two to three sentences, explain why you are reaching out to that professor. Be specific! Citing one of their articles or presentations that you found interesting, or quoting a statement about their research interest from their university, lab, or personal website would be great here. Try to make it something that is related to your research topic and explain why it interested you.

In your closing sentence of this paragraph, also try to state how you hope your research will contribute to your target supervisor's work.

Ask for a reply and the opportunity to follow-up

This is the most significant departure from the initial email from networking. Since you do not have time to develop a relationship gradually, you'll want to get a direct answer from the professor whether they can consider supervising your research and also get them to commit to a follow-up conversation about your research proposal. Make sure that your email closes with a polite, clear question or request for a reply.

That is all your email needs to include. Remember, keeping it short and to the point will make it easier for the professor to read it and reply quickly.

Attachments?

Many applicants have asked me if they should include their Field of Study and Research Program Plan as an attachment to this email. My answer is the Japanese standard: It depends.

If you have enough time before the deadline (I suggest at least a week) to follow up with the professor and talk directly, then I suggest skipping the attachment. In that situation, you want to get a reply as quickly as possible so that you can set up a call to talk about your research directly. When the professor agrees to talk to you, then you can attach your Field of Study and Research Program Plan in your follow-up email and say that you will explain it in more detail when you talk.

If the deadline is looming and you need to know right away whether to include that professor on your list or reach out to someone else, then attach the Field of Study and Research Program Plan.

Sample Message: During the Application Process

Now that you know what I recommend including in that initial email, here is a template you can follow. I have also included it in the downloadable bonus documents so that you can copy/paste it from there, but you'll need to fill in your own information!

Your field and your approach will be different, but I hope this format gives you an idea of the suggested length and contents.

* * *

Subject Line:

MEXT Scholarship Master's Degree Applicant - Request for Supervision

Body:

Dear Professor Sato,

Please pardon me for reaching out to you suddenly.

My name is Travis Senzaki and I am a bachelor's degree student in community development studies at the University of Johannesburg, South Africa. I am applying for the MEXT Scholarship in order to continue my education with a Master's degree in Environmental Policy & Rural Development studies at the Kyoto University Graduate School of Economics focused on the rehabilitation and development of former mining communities in Japan and South Africa and I have a strong desire to work under your supervision if my application is successful.

I have followed your work in the field, particularly your research on the development of the Joban Hawaiian Center in the former mining community of Iwaki, and comparisons to how other communities in Japan transitioned to a post-mining economy, from "Post-Mining Transition: A Comparison of Community Approaches in Tohoku, Japan" in the *Journal of Rural Studies.* I would like to learn more about your ongoing research and contribute to it as well while I compare the situation there with examples from my home country of South Africa.

Version 1: Contacting before submitting application

In my MEXT Scholarship application, I am required to list potential supervisors in Japan. I am interested in working under your supervision and would like to fill in your name, but I want to make sure that you would be able and willing to supervise my research if my application is successful. If you would be willing to consider it, I would be happy to send you my research proposal or arrange a call or online meeting at your convenience to talk in further detail.

Version 2: Contacting after passing the Primary Screening

I have passed the Primary Screening at the Japanese Embassy in South Africa and will be formally applying for a Letter of Provisional Acceptance shortly. I would like to work under your supervision there if you would be willing and able to consider it. If you would like, I would be happy to send you my research proposal or arrange a call or online meeting at your convenience to talk in further detail.

Could you please let me know if you could consider supervising my research and whether you would be available for a follow-up conversation? I apologize in advance for the short notice, but I need to submit my application form by [DEADLINE], so I would appreciate it very much if you could write back by that date.

Thank you in advance for your kind consideration.
Regards,
Travis

Travis Senzaki
Pronouns: He/Him/His
University of Johannesburg
BA(Hons) Community Development, Class of 2021
travis@transenzjapan.com

* * *

Notes about the example

I have used my name as the sample candidate, and the degree programs are real (as is the example of Iwaki, Fukushima), but that wasn't my academic background. Professor Sato (the most common last name in Japan) is fictional, as is the research title and journal. The point is to give an example of the level of detail you should aim for in this message and the important items to cover.

The subject line in the example is something that you can copy and use as-is, though you might want to give it your own personal touch. It's likely that multiple applicants will be reaching out to the same professor at the same time, and if more than one person is using this template, it could be difficult for the professor to keep the requests separate!

The initial greeting is a loose translation of the Japanese phrase that would be common when emailing a person who you do not know with no introduction. It may sound a little humble, but a Japanese professor should recognize it, and it will hint right away that you have some familiarity with Japanese culture.

In the first paragraph, I introduced myself, my academic background, and my MEXT scholarship candidacy. I also included the name of the specific university and graduate school to make it clear that I specifically wrote this message for that professor.

In the second paragraph, I described my interest in the professor, including his/her academic field and a specific publication. I also mentioned at the end that I hope to contribute to the professor's research. I did not go into specific detail, but the point in including that line was to show that I have an interest in contributing, not just being on the receiving end of advice.

There are two versions of the third paragraph, depending on whether you are writing before submitting the Placement Preference Form or after passing the Primary Screening. In both cases, I let the professor know where I was in the application process and what I wanted from them - as well as what they didn't need to do. I wanted to clarify that I was not asking the professor to take any action other than replying to me and discussing my research. I will handle the rest. However, I did ask to send my research proposal or arrange a meeting as soon as possible.

If you were writing this message just before the deadline and did not have time for a follow-up email or call, then I would recommend swapping out the final sentence of the third paragraph for: "I have attached my research proposal to this message and would appreciate it very much if you could take the time to look through it and see if this is something that you could supervise as-is, or with some changes. I would also be happy to discuss it with you in further detail at your convenience."

In the last paragraph, I closed with a specific question for the professor to answer and an apologetic explanation of my coming deadline. That would be the deadline to submit your application to the embassy or to apply to the university for a Letter of Provisional Acceptance, depending on your situation.

My closing greeting was thanks for the professor's time, not a request or push for a reply or any other attempt to pressure the professor. I want to leave them knowing that I appreciate the time they have given already in reading my message. Besides, I already have the question and stated the deadline above, so repeating something like "I look forward to your favorable reply" here could come across as demanding and pressuring.

As explained above, I would attach my Field of Study and Research Program to this message if there was no time to follow up, but otherwise, I would send it with no attachments.

Your turn

If you haven't done so already, it's time for you to write your first emails to your target professors. You do not need to match my template above, but try to keep your messages short and to the point, as I have done in the example, and make sure that you cover the relevant points.

There is a place in the worksheets for this, but, of course, you are free to type it directly into your email program, as well!

Once you finish, have someone else review it for clarity. Then you will be ready to hit send and move on to the next chapter, where I'll discuss how to follow up and continue to build your relationship, based on the professor's reply.

PROGRESS CHECK

You should now have a clear grasp of your communication strategy and how you want to build your relationship with each of your target professors in Japan. You also understand the specific goals for your first email and have written a draft of that message.

If you haven't done so already, have someone look over that draft to make sure that it is clear and professional then hit send!

In the next chapter, we'll be talking about the different replies - or non-replies - you might get and how to reply or respond to them. So, as soon as you've sent off your messages, read on to prepare yourself for the next steps.

EXERCISES

For this chapter, I have designed the downloadable worksheets to help you prepare for and send your first email to your prospective advisors in Japan. Some items here are simple check boxes to make sure that you have completed all the steps described throughout the chapter, but at the end, I have included my sample emails and space for you to write yours.

https://www.transenzjapan.com/mext/uniprofexercises

Email account setup

1. What email address will you be using to contact professors and universities in Japan?

2. Is this a professional-sounding email address, such as a university account or your name? Yes / No

2a. If you are setting up a new email account, do you have it set to forward to your old account, so you never miss a message that arrives? Yes / No

3. Is your sender name (the name others see in their inbox when your email arrives) your first and last name? Yes / No, but I will change it to be.

4. Do you have a signature block? Yes / No

4a. If yes, does it include:

- Your first and last name? Yes / No
- Your email address? Yes / No
- Your preferred pronouns? Yes / No
- Multiple links? Yes / No
- Links to anything you wouldn't want your professor to see, such as social media? Yes / No
- Different colored text or non-professional fonts? Yes / No
- "Sent from my smartphone", etc.? Yes / No

5. Have you set your target professor's individual email and the entire domain for your target university to your "whitelist" so that it is never filtered as spam? Yes / No

6. Have you turned off or overridden any inbox protection features, such as Boxbe? Yes / No

7. Are your replies set to always include the text of previous messages? Yes / No

8. Have you set up alerts to let you know when you have a new message, or an alarm to always check your email at a specific time of day? Yes / No

Contact information

9. What is your professor's email address?

9a. If you plan to contact the professor by phone, what is their phone number?

9b. If you could not find direct contact information for the professor, what is your strategy for reaching out to them?

Your communication strategy

10. What is your goal/the specific outcome you want from your communication with your professor?

11. What is the goal of your first email?

12. What time of day do you want your email to reach your professor?

12a. What time is that in your time zone?

Your first email

13. Write the complete draft of your first email

14. Is it a complete email with a subject line and opening and closing greetings? Yes / No

15. Is your email specific to the professor you are sending it to, mentioning them by name and including details of their research? Yes / No

16. Have you offered value to the professor in your message? Yes / No

17. Proofread your email by hand for spelling and grammar errors, or get someone else to review it for you.

18. Have someone review your email to make sure that the message is clear and ask them how they would reply if they received this message. Make sure that reply is what you are aiming for.

Once you've cleared those steps, you are ready to hit send!

CHAPTER FIVE: FOLLOW-UP CONTACT

Have you heard back from your professors yet?

Almost everything you have done as you followed along with this book so far has been under your control, but after you send off that first email, it all depends on the professor and their reply. I know this is when many applicants get most nervous. Waiting for a reply can be the hardest part of this entire application process.

Whether you are still waiting or already have your first reply, in this last chapter, we are going to look at the replies you may receive and how to respond to each.

Where you should be

At this point, you should have finished your research of universities and professors. You have thought through your communication strategy and have sent off your initial email to your first choice professors in Japan. Maybe you already have your reply, or maybe you're looking ahead to prepare what to do once that reply arrives.

From this point forward, how you communicate with your potential advisors in Japan is going to be unique to your individual circumstances. Once both of you are part of the communication process, then keep your ultimate goals and communication strategy in mind and make sure that you are replying to what the professor has to say while you move forward with your goals, as well.

In this chapter, I will cover the five major kinds of replies that you might get to your initial email, with advice about what to do in each case. Please refer to the different sections as needed.

The five types of replies

- No reply
- Refusal to reply/no contact policy
- Rejection
- Confusion
- Continued communication and acceptance

With luck, you'll only need to read about the last one, but some others might come first and it is almost certain that if you reach out to two to three professors (for the Embassy-Recommended MEXT Scholarship), at least one will not be able to supervise you (Rejection). That is perfectly normal on the road to getting accepted!

Let's look at each type of response in detail.

NO RESPONSE

If a potential supervisor does not write back to you, that is *not* a rejection! It is what I call a "No Response". The professor either hasn't seen your email yet, hasn't had time to consider your request and reply, or simply hasn't made it a priority.

What do you do in that situation? First, give them a little time, if you can afford it. But if you still don't get a reply, then it's time to analyze why that might have happened and send a polite follow-up email.

How long should you wait before a follow-up?

As a general rule, I recommend waiting one week, if you have the time. A week is appropriate, as the professor might be dealing with some other urgent matters, or might even be away from the university and checking their messages less often, depending on the time of year.

However, if a professor hasn't responded within a week, then there's a good chance that your email will now be buried in their inbox under everything else that has arrived in that time, so a polite follow-up message would be appropriate.

There are some cases where you can't afford to wait that long, particularly if you have already passed the Primary Screening and are applying for a Letter of Provisional Acceptance under a tight deadline. In that case, hopefully you indicated the deadline in your initial email! If you mentioned that deadline, then it is appropriate to follow-up again two days before the deadline with a polite reminder, even if less than a week has passed.

How to follow-up

Before writing a follow-up email to your potential advisor, consider whether your initial email was the problem.

Was your message too long? Did you have a clear call to action (request for a response) that would have made it easy for the professor to answer? Have you given the professor a good reason to want to reply - or conversely, have you given them a reason not to reply (such as a poorly prepared and written email, a poor description of your research interest, or being overly demanding of their time)?

If your email could have been the problem, then make sure that your follow-up message addresses any issues. See the previous chapter for my advice on writing that initial email.

One more step before you follow up is to check your spam mail. Yes, if you were following my advice in the previous chapter, you white-listed the professor's email address and turned off any inbox guard software, but that isn't always a perfect solution. Sometimes professors will write back from a different email address that you hadn't cleared in advance, or your whitelist filter could have a problem. It's going to be embarrassing if you send a follow-up, only to learn that the professor had already written back and was waiting on you.

Follow-up email to the professor

When writing a follow-up message, I recommend forwarding your initial email and adding a brief comment, such as the following.

* * *

Dear Prof. Sato,

Greetings again from Johannesburg, South Africa!

I was wondering if you had had time to consider the message below that I sent you last week. I am very interested in studying under you for my Master's Degree, but I would like to make sure that my research question is one that you could supervise before I move forward.

I understand you are very busy and I do not want to take up too much of your time, but I would appreciate your reply at your convenience. If you would like, I would be happy to provide more information, such as my research proposal, or arrange an online meeting to talk directly.

Thank you in advance for your consideration. I look forward to hearing from you soon.
Regards,
Travis

* * *

In the example above, I wrote "a reply at your convenience", but if you have a deadline, write that instead.

Another option, if you are in an urgent situation and have the professor's phone number, is to call them!

If the reminder doesn't get a response

You might want to reconsider whether this is a professor that you really want to work with. Even if your research has indicated that the professor is an ideal fit for your topic, your *relationship* with that professor is essential to a positive, successful experience as a MEXT scholar. Ignoring you is not a good basis for a relationship, so it may be time to consider contacting the next option on your list.

If you want to stick with this professor, though, I recommend that your next step be to contact the administrative office of the graduate school where the professor is affiliated to ask for their help. Tell them who you are, why you are contacting the professor, and what you have done so far to reach out to him or her, then ask if they could assist you in passing along a message.

Here is a template you can use for contacting the administrative office. As with the other email templates, you can find this in the downloadable bonus documents for easy copy/pasting.

In this case, I recommend you forward the messages that you have sent the professor, but also change the subject line.

* * *

Subject:

Request for Assistance Contacting Prof. Sato - Potential Master's Degree Applicant

Body:

Dear Administrative Office of the Graduate School of Economics,

Greetings from South Africa!
   I am interested in applying to your Master's Program in Economics in September 2022. I would like to study under the supervision of Professor

Taro Sato, since his research expertise is closely aligned with the research question that I want to propose.

As part of my application preparation, I have been trying to contact Prof. Sato, as shown below, to see if he could supervise my research, but I have been unsuccessful in getting a reply. I am not sure if my messages have not been delivered or if he is perhaps unavailable.

Would it be possible to ask you to pass the message below along to him?

Thank you in advance for your time and consideration. After following up with Prof. Sato, I look forward to submitting my application at the appropriate time!

Regards,
Travis

Travis Senzaki
University of Johannesburg,
BA(Hons) Community Development, Class of 2021
travis@transenzjapan.com

* * *

Even if the administrative office only ends up forwarding your email to the professor, sometimes that can increase your chances of a reply since it's coming from an internal office. I can't tell you how many times that I have seen professors bump something up on their priority list because of a reminder from a colleague or the admin office.

If the admin office knows that the professor is on sabbatical, or if there is another reason the professor cannot or will not reply (such as a no-reply policy that I will discuss in the next section), they can let you know.

Moving on to a different professor

If your reminders still do not result in a reply and you decide to give up contacting that professor to shift your attention to a new one, it is polite to let the professor know. This is particularly true if you have been contacting them after passing the Primary Screening to request a Letter of Provisional Acceptance. It is possible, if unlikely, that the professor is considering your request and, if you do not contact them, they may reply later with a Letter of Provisional Acceptance after you have moved on.

Even though the professor may not have been polite in failing to reply to your messages, there could be a legitimate reason. And as long as you pursue your academic career in that research field, there is a good chance that you will cross paths later, so wrapping up the communication can leave a positive impression that will benefit you in the long run.

When you move on to target a new professor, your final message should be concise. Write a brief email that thanks the professor for their time in considering your request, but inform them you understand they cannot supervise you as a student, so you will be considering other options. State that you still hope you will meet during your studies in Japan.

On to the next response

The "No response" is not final. Hopefully, by following the steps above, you will have changed it to one of the other four types, even if it results in rejection (or your moving on to a new professor, which is essentially the same outcome). Once you have a response of one type or another, you can move on to the next step.

REFUSAL TO REPLY/NO CONTACT POLICY

A refusal to reply differs from a "no reply". This is if the university or professor writes back to tell you they cannot or will not respond to your email at this time. There are two primary reasons this might happen.

If you get a reply like this, it is nothing personal and you should not treat it like a rejection.

A refusal to reply happens most often if you are contacting professors during the Embassy-Recommended MEXT Scholarship application process *before* you have passed the Primary Screening and it seems to be most common with private universities, including some of the best-known private universities in Japan.

Universities know that the vast majority of MEXT Scholarship applicants do not make it past the Primary Screening. In the case of private universities, they know MEXT prefers to place applicants in national universities, so there is an even lower possibility that applicants who contact them will end up studying there. Some universities decide they cannot afford to put hours of time and effort into applicants when there is realistically very little chance that they will end up studying there. It takes away from the time that they have to work with their current advisees and students. That is why these policies exist.

We both know that you're not like most applicants. That you're reading this book and following along with the exercises instantly means that you're going to be in the top percentile of applicants. You have put in a lot more preparation and thought into your application, research, and approach to your professor. But for now, you're still going to be caught up in the no-reply policy, if it exists.

What to do if the professor refuses to reply

You have two options: Wait or try elsewhere. Pushing at this point will not help. Unless you have a personal connection with the professor already, do not expect them to make a special exception to university policy for you.

I explained above why the no-reply policy makes sense from a university perspective, but you need to think about whether you want to study at a university with that kind of policy. It may indicate that the university administration will be inflexible after you arrive as well (although, to be fair, most administrative offices *are* inflexible). Of course, it doesn't mean that your relationship with your supervisor will be that way, so there is still every possibility that the professor will be personable and engaged with you once you get into contact.

If you choose to continue with that university, then list the university and professor in your Placement Preference Form for now and contact them again as soon as you pass the Primary Screening.

If you have time, it would not be a bad idea to contact the next university on your priority list, too, to see if you get a better response there. Not every university and professor that you contact is going to accept you, so it's a good idea to communicate with as many as possible to know what your chances of acceptance are. You can always put that "refusal to reply" university back on your priority list if the other professors that you contact do not work out.

No first-year advisor system

Another reason that a professor might not respond to you is if the program does not assign an advisor during the first year. I have seen at least a few programs at both the master's and doctoral level where applicants spend their first year in general coursework and select their specialization during the second year. In that case, advisors are not assigned until applicants specialize.

If you are applying to a program with this system, then you do not need to approach the professor at this point of the application. You will just apply to the administrative office of the graduate school for a Letter of Provisional Acceptance at the appropriate time. However, you still need to have a clear research proposal for the MEXT Scholarship application, so it is important to research your target advisor and know who you want to work with, even if the university will not commit to that person advising you right away.

As with the no-reply policy I described above, if you run into a university with this system, you will have to choose whether you really want to apply there. If it matters to you to be in personal contact with your advisor prior to the start of your degree, then you might want to move on to another choice. However, if you are content to wait, then there is no problem with keeping a program like this on your list.

REJECTION

Assume in advance that you are going to face rejection from at least one university or professor you contact, maybe more. Rejection is perfectly normal and there are a variety of reasons, some of which might have nothing to do with you.

In any case, rejection of your application - especially a quick rejection - can be a good thing! If you have taken the time to put together a well-developed Field of Study and Research Program Plan and planned out a thorough communication strategy, but still get rejected, it usually means that there was some kind of mismatch in your proposal and your target advisor, so it would not have been a good situation to study there.

I understand it is hard to take when it happens, but I encourage you to *embrace* rejection, to be *thankful* for it. It is just one more step toward finding the best program and advisor for you. Rejection lets you move on to the next potential advisor - and you can even contact an alternate professor at the same university in this case.

Let's look at some common reasons a professor might reject your application to study with them and what you can do in each situation.

Full lab

I'm starting with this because it can be one of the hardest reasons to accept. If a professor rejects you because they cannot take on any more advisees, then there is a chance that it might have been a good fit for you if you had applied at a different time. Unfortunately, each professor has a limited number of students they can supervise at a time, and there is really nothing that you, or they, can do if they have reached this limit except to wait for a future year. Of course, I understand that is not a realistic course of action.

If a professor writes back to say that they cannot accept you as an advisee because they have reached their limit or have a full lab, then you should first thank them for their time, then ask if they have any recommendations for an alternate supervisor. Let them know you chose them because you were interested in their research and ask if they have any colleagues - at the same university or a different one - involved in similar research that you could contact.

If they recommend another colleague, then you automatically have an advantage in that next contact because you have an introduction! However, please don't assume that they will be able or willing to do so. A personal recommendation carries a lot of weight in Japan, and it would make the recommending professor feel responsible for you to their colleague.

Retirement or resignation

I mentioned earlier in the book that around 2021, there seems to be a wave of professors retiring at many universities around Japan. A professor who plans to retire before you finish your degree will not be able to take you on as a new advisee. Similarly, if a professor is planning to change jobs at the time that you contact them, they could not accept you as an advisee.

Just like the full lab example above, if a professor cannot supervise you because they are retiring, then I recommend you ask them if they can recommend someone else that you can reach out to, instead. For example, there might be a junior professor at the same university that will take over their research or lab after they retire.

Unfortunately, the college-age population in Japan is dropping, so universities' enrollments are shrinking. That means that when a professor retires, the university might not replace them with someone in the same field. But it is still always worth your time to ask for a recommendation for other potential advisors to contact. Professors who are at retirement age should be familiar with the state of their field of research across Japan and have a broad network to offer other suggestions. The worst thing that can happen is that they do not have any suggestions, in which case it is the same as not having asked.

Not qualified to supervise

Sometimes you might reach out to a professor who is not qualified to supervise graduate students at your level. Unfortunately, it is hard to tell in advance if this is the case. Of course, professors need to have earned at least the same level degree that you are applying for (a professor who has not completed their PhD could not supervise a PhD-level student), but there are other criteria and if can vary from university to university. I am not aware of any consistent rules that apply in all cases.

As with the examples above, this is beyond your ability to change. If this happens, thank them for their reply and ask if they have any suggestions for another professor you might apply to. For example, if they are the junior professor in a lab and only lab leader can supervise, then you could still apply to that same lab and end up working with this professor, even if they aren't your official supervisor. If the professor is early in their career, they might also recommend their own previous supervisor, as well.

Research mismatch

No matter how thoroughly you have researched a target professor and tried to target your proposal to interest them, it is still possible that your research question is not a topic that they can supervise. It could be the case that the research profile you found was old, and the professor has shifted focus since then. It also happens that applicants might think that their research topic is similar enough to what the professor is working on, but the professor disagrees.

In this case, unlike the examples above, you have multiple options.

One is that you can offer to change your research to be closer to the professor's. This would be a relatively common response in STEM fields where you need to fit in to the ongoing research in the professor's lab. In that case, reply to let the professor know you are willing to shift your research to match the ongoing projects in that professor's lab, even though it does not match your original research proposal. Explain that you knew from the start that you would have to change your research to match your supervisor's but that you wanted to put together a complete research proposal as a starting point for the conversation.

The second option is, of course, to move on and contact someone else. If you are committed to your original proposal and want to research that at all costs, then you would have to continue your search.

One word of caution: There is a possibility here that the professor is saying that your research topic "doesn't match" to let you down gently. Your proposal might just not be good enough. If you get the mismatch reply from one professor, treat that is an honest reply and follow one of the steps I mentioned above. But if you find the professor isn't willing to entertain your suggestion to change your topic or if multiple professors tell you that your research doesn't match, even though you think it is similar to theirs, consider whether the quality of your research proposal might be the problem. (If you haven't done so already, see if you can get your current academic advisor or a professor at your university to evaluate it and give you feedback. I also offer a paid review service to evaluate and suggest improvements to the structure of your Field of Study and Research Program Plan, but it is better to seek the advice of someone in your research field who can comment on the content and the presentation.)

CONFUSION

"Confusion" in this case means a reply where the professor writes back to say that they are not sure what to do in response to your email. Usually, confusion relates to specific paperwork or procedures that they have to complete in order to help you get your Letter of Provisional Acceptance.

In most cases, you can avoid confusion on the professor's part by making sure that your initial email is clear and tells them what you need them to do. But sometimes professors will misread your explanation, or read more into it than you had intended. In either case, if the professor is confused, it is your responsibility to get them the information that they need. Do not assume that professors are familiar with the MEXT Scholarship application process or even that they know who to contact at their university for more information. You should look up any necessary information and walk them step-by-step through the process, if required.

How to reply to a confused professor

First, be sure to apologize for being unclear in your previous message - even if you think you were perfectly clear to begin with!

If you have not yet passed the Primary Screening and are not asking the professor for a Letter of Provisional Acceptance, then usually there is nothing official that they need to do. In that case, clarify that all you are asking for is for them to consider whether they can supervise you and your research. Tell them as well that once you get to the point of the application process when you need to ask their help with additional documentation, you will be in touch again with more details.

When you are applying for a Letter of Provisional Acceptance and need them to complete specific paperwork to support that application, be sure that you know what the process is at their university and explain it to them. The process can differ dramatically from university to university.

At some, the professor reviews your application entirely on their own and issues a Letter of Provisional Acceptance. If that is the case, you will need to send them the Letter of Provisional Acceptance template, as well as all of your application documents, and ask them to complete and return the letter to you.

Another, more common, approach is that the university will ask you to contact the professor for provisional approval, then apply to a central office. That office will then contact the professor with instructions about completing the Letter of Provisional Acceptance. If you find yourself in that situation, let the professor know that you just need their agreement to supervise your research if you are accepted for now and that the International Office (make sure you use the proper name of the office for that university!) will contact them later with further instructions.

Finally, you will find some universities that do not expect applicants to contact professors at all. They only ask you to list the professor's name and apply to the administrative office responsible for MEXT Scholars. In that case, tell the professor that there is nothing they have to do. The official application process is being handled by another office (be sure to tell them what office it is) and they will be in touch later. But explain that even though the professor does not need to take any action, that you thought it would be the polite thing to do to contact them directly to introduce yourself, first.

Hopefully, once you have resolved the "confusion" reply, your conversation will naturally flow to the next section: Acceptance.

CONTINUED COMMUNICATION AND ACCEPTANCE

Acceptance or tentative acceptance, in response to your initial email (or after going through one of the stages above), means that the professor will discuss your candidacy with you further. It does not mean that they have agreed to accept your application right away. That would be an unrealistic expectation for a first email (unless your first email to the professor was to submit your formal application). So, even after a favorable reply, you need to be prepared to continue the conversation.

This is the most time-intensive of the responses, but that's a good thing. All the effort that you put into communicating with your potential advisor now contributes to a better working relationship between you in the future.

Professional communication

Remember that your potential supervisor has never met you and can only build their impression of you through your continuing communication. You put a lot of effort into planning your first email, and you should do the same in future emails or direct conversations. Make sure that you know your goal for each message, even if it is simply to strengthen your relationship with the professor by discussing an area of mutual interest so that they are more likely to support your formal application later.

Do not relax your attention to etiquette, spelling, grammar, etc., in follow-up emails. You should continue to apply all the practices I described in the previous chapter, such as formatting your messages, including previous text, and proofreading your emails before sending. This applies even if the professor does not do the same!

If you end up communicating by video chat, such as Zoom, then make sure you are in a quiet and professional environment (use an artificial background, if you have to). Dress and prepare for the meeting as you would for an in-person job interview. Japan has high expectations for professionalism in Zoom meetings - at my university, for example, we recently had a seminar on hair, makeup, and nail care for Zoom job interviews.

Know your flexibility and deal-breaker points

As you converse with your potential advisors in Japan, they may ask you to change your research proposal. That is a good thing - it is their job to advise you and their feedback is a strong sign that they are willing to accept you as an advisee. (Do not take it as a negative sign if they do not suggest changes, they may simply be waiting until they are certain that you will study under them.)

Consider in advance how willing you are to be flexible in your research proposal. You should be willing to take on the professor's suggestions. After all, that is the whole point of earning a higher degree. If you could create a perfect research proposal now, then the degree, as well as your advisor's role, would not mean very much. However, if there is some part of your research that you are not willing to change, a "deal-breaker", know that in advance. For example, if you are committed to researching a specific example in your home country, but the professor suggests you focus on something else entirely, that might be a deal-breaker for you. If the changes exceed what you are willing to make, then you would need to consider politely ending the conversation on your end and moving on to a new potential advisor.

Once you know what your limits are for changes, let's look at some steps you might experience in the follow-up conversations.

Provide additional information

In the sample first emails that we covered in the previous chapter, typically you only described your research topic, with an offer to provide more or a request to talk directly. Once your potential advisor has responded positively, it is time to provide that information.

The professor may meet with you live over Zoom, etc., or may ask you to send your research plan or answer more questions by email. I recommend you try to accommodate the professor's preference and, in the case of live meetings, the Japanese workday. You are still the one asking them to do something for you, so try to make it easy on them. Also, even if you are meeting with them over Zoom, I recommend sending them your research proposal a day before the meeting. Tell them you will explain it when you talk, but that you wanted to provide it for their reference.

After you provide additional information, the professor may decide right away to accept you as an advisee, pending your successful application. Alternatively, they could offer suggestions for changes or decide that your research is too far from their area of expertise and that they could not supervise you, even with significant changes.

Asking for feedback

If the professor does not offer any changes or proposals after you have explained your research, it is acceptable to ask them if they have any suggestions, if you have not yet submitted your application. Let them know you are willing to make chances once you enroll and start working on your research and that you look forward to their advice then, but that you are also interested in anything they think you should change at this point, as well.

You are not entitled to their feedback or suggestions at this point in the application. Be grateful if you get it, but understand the professor may be too busy with their current advisees and research. If they say that they cannot make suggestions yet but will do so after you enroll, be sure to thank them for their feedback, anyway.

Updates on the application process

Whether your first contact with the professor is before the start of the application process or later, I recommend you keep them up to date with the major steps of your application as you move forward. For example, let them know about the following steps:

- When you submit your application to the embassy or university
- If the professor's name comes up during your interview (Embassy-Reco mmended MEXT Scholarship)
- When you get the results of the Primary Screening, whether positive or

negative
- When you submit your formal application for the Letter of Provisional Acceptance (Embassy-Recommended MEXT Scholarship)
- When you submit your Letter of Provisional Acceptance to the embassy
- When you hear any subsequent results

There may come a time when you have to inform the professor that you cannot continue your application with them. For example, if you are unsuccessful in the Primary Screening for the Embassy-Recommended MEXT Scholarship application or if MEXT places you in a different university during the Secondary Screening and University Placement process. In any of those cases, be sure to contact any potential supervisors that you have been in contact with so far to thank them for their time and let them know your next steps.

If your application is unsuccessful, let them know if you will try again and, if not, what you plan to do instead.

If you are placed at another university, let them know MEXT placed you somewhere else - tell them where - but that you appreciate their time during the application and hope that you will meet once you are in Japan at conferences or other events and that you still look forward to collaborating in the future.

Continuing the conversation

Besides the practical steps of the application process, you should continue your research on your own to prepare for your studies in Japan. I recommend you keep in contact with your potential advisors in Japan about your research progress.

If you are still enrolled in university, as you do any research related to your topic in Japan, share that with your potential advisor in Japan. Even if you are not actively researching for an ongoing degree, then you should at least be continuing to read in your field, essentially getting a head start on your literature review. If you come across interesting new ideas related to your research that might affect what you do in Japan, bring those up in conversation with your professor, as well.

I recommend you continue to keep your emails short and focused on one or two points (for example, an update in your application process as well as a reference to what you are reading currently and one to two sentences describing what you have gotten out of that work). Also, make sure to pace your emails. Of course, when you have something timely, like an application status update, you shouldn't wait to send that. But for general updates about your ongoing research, try not to send too many in a row. Wait for the professor's reply to your previous message and/or space your emails at least a week or so apart, so that you are not constantly in their inbox. Even if you are both excited about your research, it can become tiring for the professor to keep up with you too often. Consider that you are probably one of several applicants and advisees in regular contact with them, so they may have limited time to spend on each person - and nobody enjoys spending their entire day writing email!

Of course, by the time you start updating your professor on your research progress, then you are already in a great position in your relationship with them and can look forward to a successful application and studies in Japan, so you should have nothing to worry about at this point!

PROGRESS CHECK

If you have been following along with all the exercises and activities in this book, then hopefully at this point you are now in contact with at least one, if not multiple professors that you want to work with and have their support. Regardless of whether you are applying for the University-Recommende d MEXT Scholarship (to one university) or the Embassy-Recommended MEXT Scholarship (to up to three universities), any placement should be a great opportunity for your research, thanks to the work you have done in evaluating and contacting professors so far.

Remember what I said at the beginning of the book: Your relationship with your advisor in Japan is the most important consideration for the success of your studies during the MEXT Scholarship. You have done everything possible to ensure the quality of that relationship.

All that remains left for me to say is, "Good luck!" If you have put as much effort into the rest of your application as you have into this process, then I have no reason to doubt your potential for success in the MEXT scholarship application. I hope that some day, we can meet to celebrate your success in Japan!

ABOUT THE AUTHOR

Travis Senzaki is the Director of the Center for International Affairs at a university in Japan and works with international students and partner universities around the world daily.

He previously spent three years working as the first point of contact and reviewer of all MEXT scholarship applications at a large, private university, where he reviewed over 500 Embassy-Recommended and University-Reco mmended applications and answered thousands of questions.

Since moving on from that role, he launched a series of articles about the MEXT scholarship on his blog, TranSenz (https://www.transenzjapan.com/blog/mext/), and has worked with thousands more scholarship applicants through that site. His goal is to help dedicated scholarship applicants overcome confusion about the application process, reduce the role of chance in their success, and realize their dreams of studying in Japan.

He continues to follow the most recent news and application developments regarding the MEXT scholarship, as well as Japanese higher education, in English and Japanese, and shares that information with as many people as he can through the blog and his mailing list. (If you downloaded the worksheets, you are already part of that list!)

Travis is also a former international student in Japan and serves as living proof of how studying here can change the course of your life. He knew nothing about the country before arriving here as a high school student, but over the course of his year living with wonderful, supportive host families, he became passionate about Japan's history and culture and earned his master's degree in Japan Studies. Eventually, he moved back to Japan with his wife in 2011.

He is a permanent resident of Japan and lives in Akita with his wife and three children.

OTHER BOOKS BY TRAVIS

Travis writes practical manuals for living in Japan and epic fantasy novels.

Mastering the MEXT Scholarship Series

1. *How to Apply for the MEXT Scholarship*
   https://www.transenzjapan.com/mms1/
2. *How to Write a Scholarship-Winning Field of Study and Research Program Plan*
   https://www.transenzjapan.com/mms2/
3. *How to Find your Best Degree Program and Advisor for the MEXT Scholarship*
   https://www.transenzjapan.com/mms3/

Other TranSenz Guides

1. *How to Get a Spouse Visa for Japan: The TranSenz Guide*
   http://www.transenzjapan.com/spousevisa/

Epic Fantasy Novels (as T.A. Senzaki)

1. *Breyik the Apprentice*
   http://books2read.com/Breyik

REFERENCES

Google. *Google Scholar.* Last modified 2021. Accessed February 4, 2021. https://scholar.google.com/

Hokkaido University. *Divisions and Laboratories: Materials Science and Engineering.* Last modified 2021. Accessed January 25, 2021. https://www.eng.hokudai.ac.jp/e3/e3study/divisions/28-materials-science-engineering

Hokkaido University. *Syllabus and Grade Entry System.* Last modified 2021. Accessed January 27, 2021. http://syllabus01.academic.hokudai.ac.jp/Syllabi/Public/Syllabus/SylList.aspx

Hokkaido University. *Thesis/Dissertation Abstracts.* Last modified 2021. Accessed January 27, 2021. https://www.eng.hokudai.ac.jp/e3/e3alumni/abstracts

Japan Student Services Organization. *Search School.* Last modified 2021. Accessed January 6, 2021. https://www.studyinjapan.go.jp/en/planning/search-school/

Japan Study Support. *University Degree Courses in English.* Last modified 2021. Accessed January 6, 2021. http://www.jpss.jp/en/univ/english/

Martinson, Lars. *How I got the Monbusho Research Scholarship (Part 3 of 4).* Last Modified 2008. Accessed February 23, 2021. http://larsmartinson.com/how-i-got-the-monbusho-research-scholarship-part-3-of-4/

Researchmap. *Researchmap.* Last modified 2021. Accessed January 8, 2021. https://researchmap.jp/?lang=en

Saitama University. *Course Descriptions and Faculty Profiles MA Program in Japanese and Asian Culture.* Last modified 2021. Accessed January 25, 2021. http://hss.saitama-u.ac.jp/english/english_39.html

Saitama University. *Saitama University Graduate School of Humanities and Social Sciences.* Last modified 2021. Accessed January 25, 2021.

Tohoku University. *Curriculum.* Last modified 2021. Accessed January 23, 2021. https://www.econ.tohoku.ac.jp/english/page-curriculum.html

Tohoku University. *Faculty Member.* Last modified 2021. Accessed January 23, 2021. https://www.econ.tohoku.ac.jp/english/page-teacher.html

Tohoku University. *Graduate School of Economics and Management.* Last modified 2021. Accessed January 23, 2021. https://www.econ.tohoku.ac.jp/english/page-graduate.html

Tohoku University. *Regional Innovation Research Center.* Last modified 2021. Accessed January 23, 2021. https://www.econ.tohoku.ac.jp/english/page-ri rc.html

Tohoku University. *Study Fields.* Last modified 2021. Accessed January 23, 2021. https://www.econ.tohoku.ac.jp/english/page-study-field.html

Tohoku University. . Last modified 2021. Accessed January 23, 2021. https://www.econ.tohoku.ac.jp/econ/page-graduate-curriculum-curric ulum01.html

Tokyo University of the Arts. *GAP Seminar.* Last modified 2020. Accessed January 29, 2021. http://gap.geidai.ac.jp/corner83/cn9/gap_seminar_en.ht

ml

Tokyo University of the Arts. *Graduation Work and Research*. Last modified 2020. Accessed January 29, 2021. http://gap.geidai.ac.jp/corner83/cn9/graduationwork_en.html

Tokyo University of the Arts. *Hiraku Suzuki [Adjunct Instructor]*. Last modified 2020. Accessed January 31, 2021. http://gap.geidai.ac.jp/corner83/cn10/pg2061282.html

UNIV in Japan. *Home*. Last modified 2021. Accessed January 6, 2021. https://univinjapan.com/

ACKNOWLEDGEMENTS

I would like to thank Johnny Navarro who guest-posted on TranSenz about his experience in the 2020/2021 Embassy-Recommended MEXT Scholarship and also shared feedback on his experience contacting universities and professors for Letters of Provisional Acceptance.

APPENDIX: Exercises

PREPARATION EXERCISE

I highly recommend that you download the free exercise worksheets I have created, print them, and fill in the questions there as you read through the book. While some exercises might work best as a spreadsheet (I will mention that where relevant), there is something powerful about writing out your goals by hand that makes you more likely to achieve them.

https://www.transenzjapan.com/mext/uniprofexercises

Whether you handwrite or type, do not simply keep your answers to these questions in your head. Write them down. Writing your thoughts gives them power. It will help you move forward, commit to a course of action, and make progress toward your goals.

Your Goals

This is a condensed version of the exercises that appear in chapter four of *How to Apply for the MEXT Scholarship.* If you completed the exercises there, you can refer to those, instead.

1. Goals: How do you want to serve the world and society after graduation (what field of endeavor will you contribute to)?

2. Goals: What is one practical contribution to that field that you can realistically make within the first five years after graduation?

3. Goals: Visualize yourself at the point of graduation. What are you going to do next? Where will you work (or study)? What kind of work do you aim to do there?

4. Goals: What do you need to get out of your MEXT scholarship degree in order to prepare to be the version of yourself that you visualized? Make a list of the most important results to you.

5. Goals: Does your research in Japan require you to be in, or close to, a specific location in Japan?

6. Goals: Does your life situation make a particular location better for you than others? (e.g. family and cost of living, proximity to major airport, healthcare needs, living environment).

7. Goals: Start with university size, location, and ranking, and think about how each could affect your specific goals and personal situation. List the results below, then decide what factors are important to you, and how important they are. Is there anything on your list that is potentially more important to you than your relationship with your future advisor?
Size:
Location:
Ranking:

Contact Timing

8. When will your application period start? (Typically April of the year before you want to start your studies for the Embassy Application or October of the year before you want to start your studies for the University Application).

9. How much time do you have before that start date, in months?

10. Have you developed your research question? If not, when can you have that research question developed?

11. Have you finished your Field of Study and Research Program Plan? If not, when will you have that done?

12. Are you comfortable maintaining a long-distance professional relationship by email?

13. Based on all the factors above, when do you plan to contact professors?

14. Giving yourself one to three months before the contact date above, when will you research universities?

UNIVERSITY-PROFESSOR EXERCISE (UNIVERSITY FIRST)

I highly recommend that you download the free exercise worksheets I have created, especially for this chapter. These bonus worksheets include template spreadsheets for all of the lists I have described.

Basics

1. What level of degree are you applying for in Japan?

2. What field of study are you interested in applying for?

3. List at least five different ways to describe your field of study, including broader descriptions of the field and alternative ways of describing it.

University list

4. Using the websites described in this chapter, list every university and program that could include your research field. (I recommend using the downloadable spreadsheet from the bonus documents or creating your own spreadsheet for this, since you will add information to these universities as you go further with your research!)

- University Name
- Program Name
- Program Language
- Program Level
- Website

Partner university list

5. Add any partner universities in Japan to your list, including the same information as in the University List, above.

   *If the partner university is already in your University List, above, mark it with a star - you'll want to research those first!

Adding details - research relevance

In your list, add columns for the following topics.

   6. Department/Track/Major Name: Only include the one that your research topic would fall under, if appropriate.

7. Research Center: Fill in the name of any research centers related to your field of study, if applicable.

8. Relevant Courses: List any course names that apply to your research topic.

9. Instructor: For each of the courses in 8, list the name of the instructor.

10. Other Relevant Professors: Fill in the names of any other professors that might be related to your research field.

11. Program Relevance Rating: As explained in Step 2, rank the program's relevance to your research interest on a "Yes/Maybe/No" scale. For any "No", you can cross them off your list (or hide the row, if you are working with the template spreadsheets). You will not need to research them any further.

Adding details - goal relevance

Only add and research the following columns if you have already decided that they are important to your research and graduation goals. Refer to questions 4-7 in the Chapter 1 Exercise and only look up those items.

12. Size (Optional): Fill in the number of students for the university and for the graduate school, including the number of international students.

13. Location (Optional): Fill in the city where the university is located.

14. Rank (Optional): Fill in the university's ranking - be sure to use the same ranking system for all universities, if available. You can't compare rankings between systems!

15. Goal Relevance Rating: If you filled in any of the columns above, give each university a ranking on the "Yes/Maybe/No" scale. However, unlike the Research Relevance ranking above, I do not recommend that you eliminate any universities from your list based on a "No" here, unless it truly is a deal breaker and you would rather have no MEXT Scholarship at all, rather than

studying there!

Relationships

You should have already starred any universities where you have an official partnership, so this is for unofficial partnerships.

16. Mark any university where you have a personal relationship or a potential personal relationship with a star - or a second star, if you also have an official partnership.

17. Fill in the name and contact information of your connection with that university.

Professor profile

18. Create a new list for professors, or use the spreadsheet in the bonus worksheets, and fill in the information below for each potential advisor you are interested in at each of the universities remaining on your list.

- Name
- Rank (Professor, Associate Professor, Assistant Professor, Lecturer, etc.)
- Sex
- Department
- Area of research interest
- Courses taught
- Lab name/website (if applicable)
- Any international faculty/students in lab? (yes/no)
- Personal website (if applicable)
- Most recent publication title, date, and language
- Most recent presentation title, date, and language

- Common subject themes in recent publications/presentations
- Most recent update to personal website/lab website/researchmap profile
- Date earned bachelor's degree
- Estimated date of retirement ((date of bachelor's degree)+38 years)
- Email/phone number (if possible)

The final university-professor pair list

19. Make one final list of the remaining universities and one first-choice professor at each, including the information below:

- University Name
- Graduate School Name
- Professor Name
- Program Website
- MEXT Scholarship Application Information Page
- Professor's Contact Information

UNIVERSITY-PROFESSOR EXERCISE (PROFESSOR FIRST)

Most of the work that you will do in this chapter works best in a spreadsheet and I have included a template in the downloads.

Basics

1. Brainstorm a list of all the potential keywords related to your research that you can use to search for potential advisors in Japan.

Potential advisor list

I recommend using the spreadsheet you can download from the link above for this process, but if you don't want to use that sheet, you can make your own list, starting with the columns below.

- Name
- Research focus area
- Name of affiliated university & graduate school
- Link to personal profile or website
- Contact information

2. From your previous literature review, identify all the authors in the works you reviewed who are affiliated with Japanese universities and add them to your list. (Just the names, for now.)

3. Go through the citations from the works in your literature review and add any authors of relevant cited works who teach at universities in Japan. (Again, just the names.)

4. Search Researchmap using the keywords in question 1, above, and check the profiles of each researcher from the search results. Add any that have similar research fields to your own to your list.

5. Review journals and e-journals in your field from the past year and read the abstracts of any articles related to your research that you find. Research the authors of those articles and add them to your list if they are affiliated with a Japanese university.

6. Google your keywords from question 1, along with the words "university Japan". If you find any new faculty members at Japanese universities researching in your field, add them to your list.

7. Consult with your personal network for any additional names of researchers in your field who are active in Japan. Research those faculty members and add them to your list. Mark a star next to these researchers' names to show that you have a network connection to them for potential introduction later.

Advanced faculty research

8. Add the columns below to your table of potential advisors and use Researchmap, Google Scholar, or their personal websites to fill in the information, if possible:

- Number of publications or presentations in last three years
- Percentage of publications or presentations in English
- Number of citations in last five years (Google Scholar)
- Years since bachelor's degree
- Rank (Professor/Associate Professor, etc.)
- Similar thesis topics among advisees (yes / no)

University program research

9. Add a "Program Language" column to your table and record whether the program is offered in English or Japanese.

10. If the program is taught in Japanese but there is a related program offered in English where you could enroll and still work with that supervisor, add a column for "Related English Program" and write the name of the program taught in English. Research a potential advisor in that program and add that professor to your list as a separate entry, filling in all the relevant details from the questions above.

Prioritize

11. If using a spreadsheet, add a "Rank" column to your list (I recommend adding it on the left) and prioritize your potential supervisors in the order that you think you would like to work with them. If you are not using a spreadsheet, I recommend creating a new list, where you include only the information below. Write your professors in that list in your priority order.

- University Name
- Graduate School Name
- Professor Name
- Program Website
- MEXT Scholarship Application Information Page
- Professor's Contact Information

INITIAL CONTACT EXERCISE

Don't forget, I have included my email templates in the downloadable bonus documents for easy reference, as well!

Email account setup

1. What email address will you be using to contact professors and universities in Japan?

2. Is this a professional-sounding email address, such as a university account or your name? Yes / No

2a. If you are setting up a new email account, do you have it set to forward to your old account, so you never miss a message that arrives? Yes / No

3. Is your sender name (the name others see in their inbox when your email

arrives) your first and last name? Yes / No, but I will change it to be.

4. Do you have a signature block? Yes / No

4a. If yes, does it include:

- Your first and last name? Yes / No
- Your email address? Yes / No
- Your preferred pronouns? Yes / No
- Multiple links? Yes / No
- Links to anything you wouldn't want your professor to see, such as social media? Yes / No
- Different colored text or non-professional fonts? Yes / No
- "Sent from my smartphone", etc.? Yes / No

5. Have you set your target professor's individual email and the entire domain for your target university to your "whitelist" so that it is never filtered as spam? Yes / No

6. Have you turned off or overridden any inbox protection features, such as Boxbe? Yes / No

7. Are your replies set to always include the text of previous messages? Yes / No

8. Have you set up alerts to let you know when you have a new message, or an alarm to always check your email at a specific time of day? Yes / No

Contact information

9. What is your professor's email address?

9a. If you plan to contact the professor by phone, what is their phone number?

9b. If you could not find direct contact information for the professor, what is your strategy for reaching out to them?

Your communication strategy

10. What is your goal/the specific outcome you want from your communication with your professor?

11. What is the goal of your first email?

12. What time of day do you want your email to reach your professor?

12a. What time is that in your time zone?

Your first email

13. Write the complete draft of your first email

14. Is it a complete email with a subject line and opening and closing greetings? Yes / No

15. Is your email specific to the professor you are sending it to, mentioning them by name and including details of their research? Yes / No

16. Have you offered value to the professor in your message? Yes / No

17. Proofread your email by hand for spelling and grammar errors, or get someone else to review it for you.

18. Have someone review your email to make sure that the message is clear and ask them how they would reply if they received this message. Make sure that reply is what you are aiming for.